BURLINGTON

THE CENTRAL GOVERNMENT WAR HEADQUARTERS AT CORSHAM

BURLINGTON

THE CENTRAL GOVERNMENT WAR HEADQUARTERS AT CORSHAM

Nick Catford

FOLLY BOOKS

A catalogue record for this book is available from the British Library.

ISBN 978-0-9564405-6-3

Published by Folly Books Ltd
Monkton Farleigh
BA15 2QP
www.follybooks.co.uk

Designed and typeset by Vicky

Printed and bound in India by Replika Press Pvt Ltd.

Jacket and introductory photographs
Front jacket: The manual trunk telephone exchange in the Central Government War Headquarters.
Back jacket: Maintenance vehicle parked on East Main Road near passenger lift PL2.
Facing title page: Double blast doors and air-lock at the top of PL2 lift shaft. This would be the first view of the Central Government War Headquarters seen by government officials when they arrived at BURLINGTON.
Facing Chapter 1: A view to the east along East Main Road.

PREFACE

Peter Morgan's words, spoken with the tacit agreement of senior Ministry of Defence personnel escorting a Channel Four television film crew in the underground labyrinth at Corsham, were hugely significant, for they represented the first public acknowledgement by the British Government, after almost forty years of vehement denial, of the existence and true function of an enormous underground bunker known as the Central Government War Headquarters, buried deep beneath the north Wiltshire countryside.

The ostensible purpose of the visit was to publicise the fact that the Ministry of Defence was putting onto the open market the redundant Admiralty underground storage depot known as RNSD Spring Quarry at Corsham. The site extended over some two million square feet and appeared to have considerable potential commercial value. The storage depot was a post-war development of a wartime underground factory that had itself been constructed within a worked-out and abandoned stone mine in the early years of the Second World War. The proposed sale was in some respects a risky proposition, for not all of the wartime factory had been converted into storage space for the Admiralty in the 1950s; to the northwest of the site more than a million square feet had been partitioned off for another highly secret purpose. Three sets of massive, blast-proof doors, installed as emergency fire exits, joined the two areas and they would prove difficult to explain these away to any prospective purchaser. A credible explanation would perhaps have been even more difficult had

they known that just a few years earlier each door was guarded by an armed serviceman.

The film crew, along with Peter Morgan, the investigative journalist Duncan Campbell, and military historian Nick McCamley were scheduled to arrive at Corsham at 10 o'clock on a wet Wednesday morning in November and the day was to begin with a health and safety briefing in the Property Services Agency offices there. One member of the group arrived somewhat earlier, however, and after the offer of coffee became involved in a deep discussion with the PSA maintenance staff and a member of the RAF police force who were to act as escorts during the visit. A little while later, before the rest of the film crew arrived, a senior Ministry of Defence official burst into the room and made a comment along the lines of: 'right lads, the media people will be here in a quarter of an hour. When we take them underground we're staying at the bottom of the depot, we're going nowhere near the BURLINGTON doors, (BURLINGTON being an obsolete but widely used code-name for the Central Government War Headquarters), as far as we're concerned and as far as they are concerned, BURLINGTON does not exist and we know nothing about it.' With a rapidly identified stranger in their midst, the MoD contingent collapsed briefly into confusion. Nevertheless, the visit went ahead although, initially at least, suffused by an atmosphere of brittle tension. After two hours or so of desultory filming, during which the MoD tried valiantly to maintain the fiction of a non-existent bunker to the north while fending off frequent prodding from the television crew asking the question 'well this is sort-of interesting but what about the doors to BURLINGTON?' they suddenly, and to everyone's amazement, caved in completely. The senior MoD official who just a few hours earlier had so resolutely determined that no mention at all should be made of BURLINGTON muttered 'Oh just show them the doors and be done with it!' And that, to all intent and purpose, was the end of the BURLINGTON secret. Shortly after the programme was broadcast the story was taken up by the local and national press, culminating in a full-page illustrated feature in the *Guardian* which included conjectural but, as it later transpired, remarkably accurate plans of the bunker.

Efforts were made by the government to suppress interest in the story but, despite their tight-lipped and obstinate silence, it was too late to undo what had been done. The fact was, however, that throughout this period the Cabinet Office was slowly coming to the conclusion that the Corsham bunker was an anachronism and its days were inevitably numbered. The possibility of declassifying the site was first discussed and then agreed at a Machinery of Government in War Committee meeting in October 2004. Following that meeting a case was made and approval given for declassification. Quietly, to arouse the minimum press attention, this decision was made public on Christmas Eve 2004. Later that day the MoD announced on an obscure page of its website that:

'A formerly secret government underground site near Corsham in Wiltshire, which was a potential relocation site for the government in the event of a nuclear war, was declassified at the end of 2004.'

Despite the change in classification, almost fifty years of rigorous secrecy had created a mind-set amongst staff involved with the Corsham headquarters that resisted change. Although visits by the press and a few other interested parties were arranged they were accompanied by a distinct atmosphere of grudging unwillingness. Reasons were sought to refuse or limit the scope of visits to the underground areas and a Press Brief was prepared listing likely questions that might be asked by journalists, and detailing bland and evasive replies that might be given. Some were contradictory. It was stated, for example, that many areas were out-of-bounds because of health and safety concerns while the answer to a question regarding

the on-going maintenance cost was that over the past ten years the annual expenditure had been in the region of £500,000. In a letter to the Defence and Overseas Secretariat with reference to the Press Brief, a concerned MoD official commented:

'A question springs to mind … If we have spent money maintaining Site 3, (the Central Government War Headquarters), surely the site manager will not be able to debar visitors on health and safety grounds otherwise what have we got for our £5 million?'

Despite its historic significance, declassification did not result in an immediate cascade of hitherto top-secret documents into the public domain, revealing the policies behind the establishment of the CGWHQ at Corsham, of its construction and evolution over its forty-year lifetime or of the procedures that would have governed its functioning had it ever become operational. This reticence to reveal is perhaps understandable, for many of the assumptions upon which its role and function were predicated – certainly by the early 1970s – are to an extent still relevant today. Over the following seven years, however, many of the secrets *were* gradually revealed, pried rather reluctantly from the Cabinet Office using as a lever the surprisingly effective Freedom of Information Act. Much of the credit for this work is due to two assiduous researchers, Steve Fox and Mike Kenner upon whose painstaking revelations much of the text of this book is based and to whom a great debt of gratitude is acknowledged.

A note on the Area plans:
The plans that precede the photographs of each Area in the final section of this book are based upon the original and most comprehensive layout agreed in 1959. Due to the constantly fluctuating status of the headquarters some of the construction work required to comply with this original layout was never completed and in some places what are designated on the plans as specific departmental offices are no more than anonymous partitioned rooms devoid of fixtures, fittings, features or character. The plans, in short, show what might have been while the accompanying photographs show what is today. After 1968 some areas were abandoned completely while others underwent considerable change. When dealing with the latter areas plans are included showing the layouts both before and after the alterations were made.

Within the headquarters all the pillars that support the roof structure are prominently marked in red paint with a unique identifying number. Wherever possible, pillar numbers visible in the accompanying photographs have been marked on the relevant plans in order that the reader might identify the viewpoint from which the photograph was taken.

CONTENTS

		Page
1	INTRODUCTION	1
2	SUBTERFUGE	13
3	ENTRANCES & EXITS	49
4	THE AREAS	65
	Area 1 Old Telephone Exchange & West Plant Room	66
	Area 2 1961–1968 Government Departments	72
	1968–2004 RAF Quarry Operations Centre	74
	Areas 3, 4 & 5 Dormitories	79
	Areas 6 & 7 Canteen, Kitchen & Industrial Bakery	82
	Area 8 Telephone Exchange	90
	Area 9 The Stores	109
	The Hospital	122
	Area 10 Ministry of Transport	128
	Area 11 Plant Rooms & Workshops	133
	Area 12 Canteen, Kitchen & Laundry	152
	Area 13 Ministries of Food and Power	166
	Area 14 War Cabinet	168
	Areas 15 & 16 Establishment Sections & Home Departments	174
	Area 17 VIP Accommodation	184
	Area 18 The Armed Services	192
	Area 19 The Power House	194
	Area 20 Industrial Laundry	199
	Area 21 Communications Centre	202
	Area 22 Foreign & Commonwealth Departments	214
	BIBLIOGRAPHY	216

Chapter 1

INTRODUCTION

This is the story of the Central Government War Headquarters at Corsham. For almost fifty years the secret underground headquarters, (frequently referred to in recent years as BURLINGTON due to the chance discovery in 1997 by the investigative journalist Duncan Campbell of one of its numerous code-names), was the most mysterious, sensitive and secret government site in Britain. It was from this complex of offices and dormitories, conference rooms, map rooms, canteens and kitchens, communications centres and plant rooms, sprawling beneath some eighty acres of the north Wiltshire countryside, that Britain and her diminished empire would have been governed should London have become untenable in the event of a nuclear war with the Soviet Union. It was from here, too, that under certain circumstances nuclear retaliation would have been authorised and from where, in co-operation with a network of dispersed Regional Seats of Government, the nation's slow recovery from the aftermath of nuclear war would be overseen and co-ordinated.

From its inception the Corsham project was bedevilled by paranoid Whitehall secrecy and by Treasury parsimony. A mere handful of senior civil servants, and few politicians other than the Prime Minister, were ever privy to the Corsham secret; none of the four thousand or so men and women of lesser rank in the government hierarchy, secretly earmarked to operate the headquarters in event of war, had any inkling of the existence of the Corsham bunker, or of their predestined roles within it. All the shackles that this obsessive secrecy imposed upon the smooth running of the project, from the planning phase, through construction and the establishment of communications links, to the point at which the headquarters could be brought to a state of readiness, are explained in detail in the pages that follow. Before we begin a detailed examination of the Central Government War Headquarters, however, it is necessary, in order to fully understand the rationale behind Britain's plans for maintaining the continuity of government during and after a nuclear attack, to look at the earlier history of not just the Corsham site but also of a number of other locations in London and in the provinces, all of which experienced their birth pangs during the lead-up to the Second World War.

By 1934 the British government was sure that another major war was looming upon the horizon and, despite the general leaning towards a policy of appeasement, began to make preparations, if not for war, then for effective measures of passive defence. During the 1930s military air power became increasingly significant. Indeed, the most sinister threat to Britain's security, (a threat grossly exaggerated as it later transpired), identified by the country's military strategists was that posed by the German air force. Within hours of the declaration of war, they confidently predicted, the skies over London would blacken with German bombers, the capital would be obliterated, the seat of government destroyed and it would be the end of England and the end of the British Empire. On a more positive note, however, it was estimated that although the Germans possessed an overwhelming numerical superiority in bomber aircraft (and, according to Prime Minister Stanley Baldwin, 'the bomber would always get through'), those bombers had only a limited range and, flying from air bases within Germany, could reach only London and the Home Counties. Within this vulnerable area were located many culturally important institutions along with strategically vital military establishments, factories essential to the war effort and the headquarters of many businesses pivotal to Britain's economic and industrial survival. A series of complex evacuation plans developed from 1934 were designed to safeguard these vital institutions.

Most important in the context of this book was a scheme to relocate the British Army's war reserves of ammunition which were currently stored at Woolwich Arsenal and in a sprawling, surface ammunition depot at Bramley near Basingstoke, both located well within the designated vulnerable area. From the outset, the War Office decided upon a 'belt-and-braces' approach to finding a solution to their problem. First, a notional line was drawn from the Wash to the Solent, and the areas north and west of that line declared invulnerable to bombing. Not only would the ammunition stocks be relocated on the safe side of the Wash-Solent line, however, they would also be housed deep underground. Eventually, after a protracted search, underground accommodation suitable for conversion was found in a vast network of worked-out subterranean stone quarries in north Wiltshire, in and around the town of Corsham. All of these quarries were owned by the Bath & Portland Stone Company and by the end of 1937 two major groups of workings at Monkton Farleigh and Eastlays, along with Tunnel Quarry which lay north of and immediately adjacent to Brunel's Box railway tunnel, were purchased from the company. The old quarries worked a bed of oolitic limestone that was found approximately 100 feet below ground and occurred in beds between twelve and thirty feet in depth. A year or so after the War Office made its first foray underground the Air Ministry began a similar exercise developing quarries elsewhere in the country for use as underground reserve bomb stores and later still the Admiralty, with some misgivings, also began construction of underground ammunition storage depots. None of these, however, need concern us unduly. By the end of 1938 construction at all these locations was well under way and it appeared that the government's portfolio of subterranean real estate was complete.

When war was declared in September 1939 the expected aerial attack did not materialise, but another of the 1934 evacuation procedures swung into action. This was a scheme developed by the Museums and Galleries Air Raid Precautions Committee, brought into being by the Treasury and seen through to fruition by Kenneth Clarke, the Director of the National Gallery. Detailed plans had been prepared for the evacuation of all the contents of the various museums and art galleries in London to forty pre-allocated country houses in the 'safe' areas of Britain, the owners of which, purely out of patriotism, had agreed to take custody of the artefacts. The evacuation, meticulously planned, worked faultlessly but in the spring of 1940 everything changed. France capitulated, the German army over-ran northern France and the Luftwaffe occupied all the airfields on France's channel coast. From these locations their aircraft could range across the length and breadth of England rendering the whole of the previously 'safe' area suddenly vulnerable to aerial bombardment. This had serious repercussions for the Museums and Galleries Air Raid Precautions Committee. The owners of the country houses participating in the evacuation scheme were already on the point of rebellion at being confronted by the Treasury with the costs and responsibilities of housing the nation's treasures, and now those houses were at risk of destruction from the air. Probably

Below: The green overlay indicates the full extent of the Clift and Spring Quarry underground workings at Corsham. The area occupied by the Central Government War Headquarters (BURLINGTON) is indicated in pink.

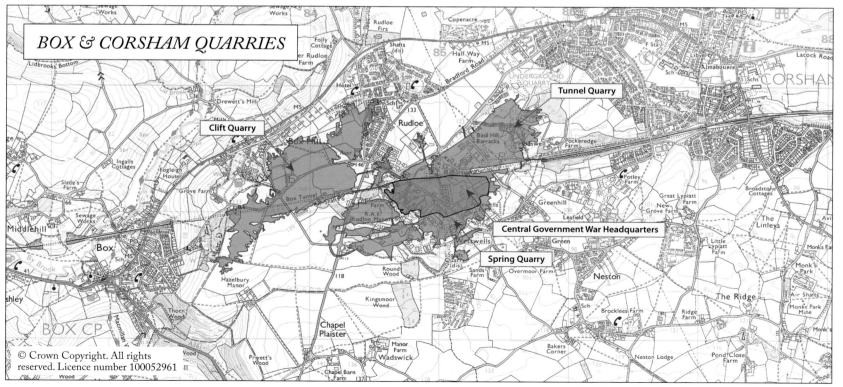

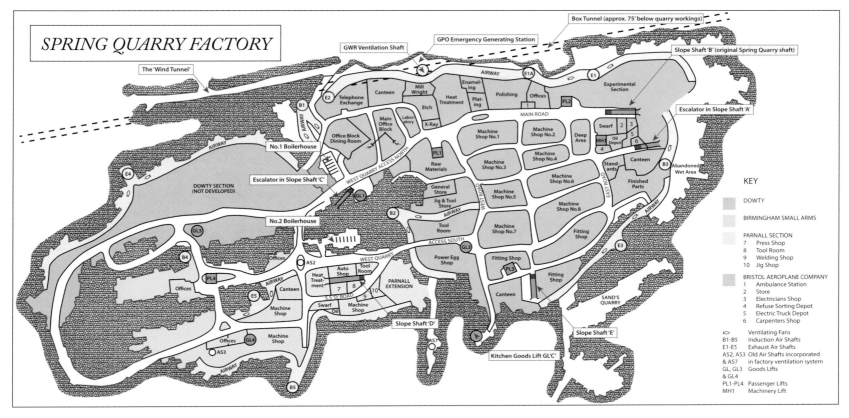

SPRING QUARRY FACTORY

KEY

DOWTY

BIRMINGHAM SMALL ARMS

PARNALL SECTION
7 Press Shop
8 Tool Room
9 Welding Shop
10 Jig Shop

BRISTOL AEROPLANE COMPANY
1 Ambulance Station
2 Store
3 Electricians Shop
4 Refuse Sorting Depot
5 Electric Truck Depot
6 Carpenters Shop

⊂⊃ Ventilating Fans
B1-B5 Induction Air Shafts
E1-E5 Exhaust Air Shafts
AS2, AS3 Old Air Shafts incorporated
& AS7 in factory ventilation system
GL, GL3 Goods Lifts
& GL4
PL1-PL4 Passenger Lifts
MH1 Machinery Lift

of more importance, however, was the fact that all the RAF airfields, upon which Britain's defence relied, were now vulnerable and, even more importantly, so were the factories that supplied the RAF with aircraft and replacement engines. In November 1940 Lord Beaverbrook, the Minister of Aircraft Production, ordered that alternative underground factories should be constructed to house the entire British aircraft industry within six months. Beaverbrook was quickly told that his plan was not feasible; there was not sufficient existing underground accommodation available, and to excavate purpose-built tunnels would take years rather than months, even if the funds were available to do so, which they were not. Nor were there the materials to build and fit-out the proposed factories. In the light of this, the scope of Beaverbrook's plan contracted significantly and only two major factory schemes and a handful of minor ones were initiated. Two of these factory sites, redeveloped during the Cold War years, figure prominently in this book, and one other just marginally.

The largest of the underground factories, encompassing an underground area of 3,300,000 square feet, was constructed in Spring Quarry at Corsham. The Bath & Portland Stone Company

Above: Schematic layout of the Bristol Aeroplane Company's underground factory at Spring Quarry. The general layout of roadways and services was retained when the site was redeveloped as the CGWHQ.

was still working Spring Quarry in November 1940 when it was peremptorily requisitioned by the Ministry of Aircraft Production. All their remaining quarries in north Wiltshire which had not already been purchased by the various Service Departments during the pre-war years were also requisitioned as a precautionary measure. Most remained unused although parts of Westwood Quarry, near Bradford-on-Avon, were developed as a factory for the Royal Enfield Company who manufactured precision instruments, including bomb-sights for the Air Ministry and gun-sights and anti-aircraft gun predictors for the War Office. A further section of Westwood Quarry was handed over to the Museums and Galleries Air Raid Precautions Committee, and within it, by the end of 1941, was concentrated all the treasures previously dispersed in its country houses with the exception of the pictures from the National Gallery. These 2,000 paintings subsequently found refuge in Manod Quarry, a disused slate working deep beneath the Snowdon mountains in North Wales.

Above: The girl in the foreground is assembling valve gear for a Bristol Hercules engine while the young lady in the background is working on a series of cylinder heads.

The conversion of Spring Quarry into an alternative production facility for Hercules engines, manufactured by the Bristol Aeroplane Company, over-stretched the capacity of the Ministry of Aircraft Production and of the Ministry of Works who shouldered overall management of the project. It was estimated that the factory would be completed within six months at a cost of £100,000 and that after completion it would produce 260 Hercules engines per month. In fact, building was still incomplete at the end of the war, construction costs had risen to £13,000,000 with a further £30,000,000 required for machine tools and other plant, and no Hercules engines were ever built there. By the time the factory was ready for production the threat of bombing had become negligible and the Bristol Aeroplane Company was distinctly unwilling to transfer its production facilities from its factory at Filton, near Bristol, to the congested and inefficient plant built for them at Spring Quarry. Eventually, the company agreed to establish a development plant and pilot production line for its new, eighteen-cylinder Centaurus engine in the quarry. Eventually 523 engines were built there, many of which failed under test, the high failure rate blamed primarily upon the inadequate working conditions in the quarry. Each engine assembled at Spring Quarry

absorbed 240 man-months, while identical engines manufactured at a conventional surface factory at Accrington required only twenty-nine man-months for completion. At the end of the war, after a few months during which the Bristol Aeroplane Company briefly took a disastrously tangential approach to turbine engine development at the Corsham site, the factory was quickly closed down, having by then become an embarrassment to all concerned.

Despite its deficiencies, the Spring Quarry factory was a prodigious and spectacular undertaking. Although it was originally intended that the Bristol Aeroplane Company should occupy all of the 3,300,000 square feet available, a number of policy changes resulted in the company eventually taking up only the eastern half of the quarry. Subsequently the Birmingham Small Arms Company established a barrel mill in the southwest quadrant, manufacturing Hispano cannon barrels, while the Dowty company of Gloucester expressed an interest in the northwest quadrant which they intended to fit-out as a factory to manufacture undercarriage legs for the Short Stirling bomber. This latter scheme was abandoned when it was discovered that the ceiling height was too low to accommodate the

Below: A small lathe set up in the development section of the Spring Quarry factory. Note the early installation of fluorescent lighting.

Above: Plan showing locations of principal underground sites referred to in this book.

finished product and no adaptation work, other than the clearance of a certain amount of quarry waste, was ever undertaken there. Despite these curtailments, services provided to the site were based upon full occupancy. The original forecast estimated a workforce of 25,000 (subsequently reduced to 12,500) and sufficient means of ingress and egress were provided to cope with this number in the short period of time required for shift changes. This rapid movement of personnel was to be achieved by means of four high-capacity vertical passenger lifts and two Otis escalators fitted in inclined shafts at the east and west extremities of the factory. When it was found impossible to acquire new escalators due to the strictly prioritised allocation of metals to the armament industry, the Ministry of Works requisitioned two London Transport escalators from Holborn and St. Paul's tube stations which were then dismantled and transferred to Corsham. Raw materials and finished products were transported between surface and underground via four twenty-ton goods lifts and two dedicated machinery lifts, which were essentially twenty-ton capacity chain hoists mounted on gantries above vertical concrete

shafts. Eight very extensive canteens and restaurants were provided to feed the entire workforce on a three shift basis. The restaurants were decorated with striking, individually themed floor-to-ceiling murals painted by a theatrical designer named Olga Lehmann, who later achieved considerable fame, including an Oscar nomination, for her post-war film sets and costume design. A dedicated lift was installed just to deliver food to the underground kitchens while two more were installed to remove ash from the boilerhouses.

Ventilation was achieved by means of twenty-one vertical air shafts and fifteen enormous axial flow induction, exhaust and circulating fans, the largest of which was fifteen feet in diameter. Fresh air drawn either from the vertical shafts or from the surrounding old quarry workings was blown via steam-heated radiators into under-floor ducts, many of which were more than eight feet in height, traversing beneath the floors of the factory and provided at intervals with up-stands or outlets which allowed fresh, warm air to circulate within the workshops and roadways. Stale air was extracted via high-level trunking connected to a floor-to-ceiling exhaust air drift that ran around the northern and eastern perimeters of the factory.

As we shall see in greater detail below, the Spring Quarry site remained in government ownership at the end of the war and in the 1950s it became a key element of the Cold War continuity of government contingency plans.

A smaller but equally sophisticated underground factory was constructed within tunnels excavated in virgin ground at Drakelow near Kidderminster in 1941. Here, into a sandstone hillside on the Blakeshill estate, four 1,000-foot-long parallel tunnels approximately 250 feet apart and eighteen feet in height were bored to provide main access routes into the factory. Closely spaced cross-passages were then excavated between the main tunnels to provide workshops, machine shops, stores and offices. Further excavations were later made adjoining the north of the main area where a further group of entrance tunnels pierced the hillside at a right angle to the main access routes. Operated as a Shadow Factory by the Rover Car Company, the factory's main output was components for the Bristol Hercules aero engine. Full production was achieved in May, 1943 when some 600 people were employed there. Although aircraft engine production ceased at Drakelow at the end of the war, Rover continued to occupy the site for almost a decade, manufacturing engines and components for the automotive industry. Drakelow reverted to full government control in 1955, by which time it, too, was earmarked for a role in the emergency government programme.

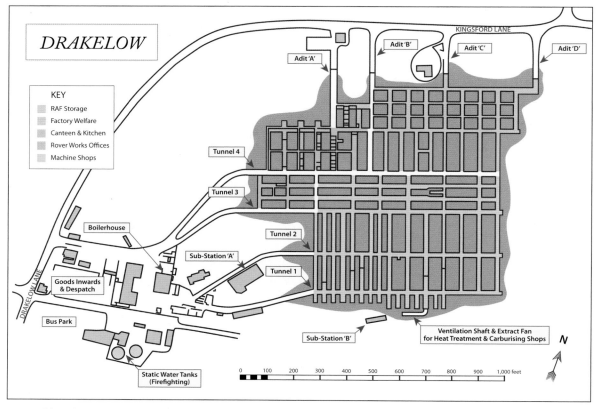

Above: The approach to No.1 tunnel, with its ventilation tower in the foreground.

Above: Plan showing the layout of the tunnels at Drakelow.
Below left: The entrance to No.2 tunnel.

Below right: A typical workshop area in the northern section of the Drakelow underground factory.

The final underground wartime industrial site to concern us is the somewhat sinister system of tunnels at Rhydymwyn, near Mold in North Wales. Shortly before the outbreak of war in 1939, here, in the Alyn Valley, work began, under the aegis of the chemical manufacturer Imperial Chemical Industries Ltd's Special Products Division, on the construction of a plant for the synthesis of mustard gas and other military vesicants. Production began in January 1941. Into the hillside to the north of the factory a system of tunnels was bored to store the output of the Rhydymwyn factory, generally referred to as 'Valley Works', and the greater part of the output of another group of chemical weapons factories already in production in the Runcorn area on the Mersey estuary. Three entrance tunnels approximately 550 feet in length and 250 feet apart were bored into the hillside and four larger transverse tunnels, varying in length between 482 feet and 770 feet, were constructed between them to provide storage chambers. Production ceased on 4 May 1945 but the tunnels remained in use for the storage of Britain's residual chemical weapons stockpile until May 1960, after which they were cleared and decontaminated. Subsequently this site too was earmarked for a role in the Cold War emergency government plans.

Above: The entrance to the middle, or No.2, tunnel at Rhydymwyn.

Right: Aerial view of the Rhydymwyn factory, with the outline of the underground storage tunnels beneath the hillside to the north outlined in pink. 'Pyro' and 'Runcol' were types of mustard gas with different physical characteristics. Before the factory was fully commissioned the demand for chemical weapons was scaled back and the P6 Pyro plant was never fitted out with its production plant. Instead, it became a highly secret pilot plant for the separation of Uranium isotopes as part of the Anglo-American atomic bomb project, using an experimental gaseous diffusion method devised by Professors Simon and Peierls.

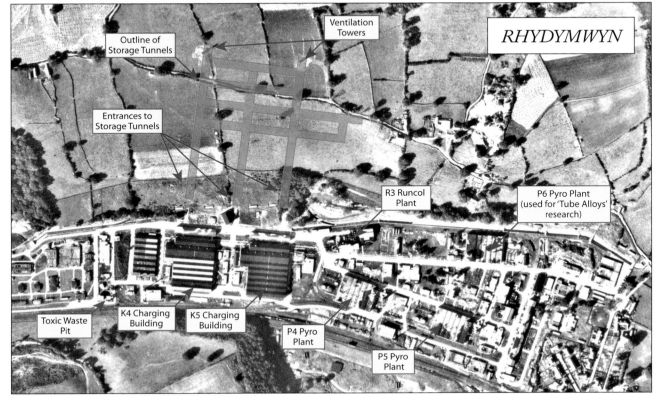

Plans for the survival of Central Government

During the inter-war years the perceived vulnerability of London and the seat of government led in 1936 to the formation of a committee chaired by the head of the Civil Service, Sir Warren Fisher, which proposed plans to evacuate the greater part of the Whitehall civil service establishment to the relative safety of the West Country, northwest England and the Midlands. A core of key civilian and military staff, consisting of some 12,000 personnel, would remain in London but would be relocated to protected accommodation in the northwest suburbs of the city. With war looming in 1938 following the Munich Crisis, the Warren Fisher scheme, which had met with general approval from the cabinet in February 1937, was taken up by the Rae committee, chaired by a senior Treasury official Sir James Rae, and handed on to the Office of Works, forerunner of the Ministry of Works and Building, who began to make detailed preparations.

Above: Exterior view of the HM Stationery Office printing works in Wealdstone. The Air Ministry War Room is buried beneath the courtyard in the foreground. Ventilation towers for the underground bunker can be seen flanking the central bay of the surface building.

It was envisaged that five underground war rooms would be built in the Harrow area, for the RAF, Admiralty, War Office, War Cabinet and Ministry of Home Security. Principal staff and executive functions would be concentrated in the war rooms whilst ad-hoc surface accommodation nearby would be found for the lesser administrative functions and to house junior staff.

The Air Ministry War Room, known as STATION Z, was constructed to the rear of the HM Stationery Office printing works at Headstone Drive in Wealdstone. It consisted of a two-storey underground bunker beneath a courtyard surrounded on all four sides by a three-storey brick office complex. The upper floor of the bunker was protected by three-and-a-half feet of reinforced concrete, the lower level by a further six feet of concrete.

Above: The long abandoned and partially flooded lower floor of STATION Z, the Air Ministry War Room at Headstone Drive in Wealdstone. Note the massive concrete pillars supporting the floor above.

Plans for an underground War Office bunker at Hounslow were replaced by an alternative scheme to construct a War Room beneath Kneller Hall in Twickenham, an eighteenth century mansion acquired by the War Office in 1856 and used, up until the Second World War and beyond, as the home of the Royal Military School of Music.

Although an underground War Room in the Harrow area was proposed for the Ministry of Home Security in 1938 the plan was subsequently abandoned and the department was compelled to make do, during the early war years, with accommodation in the strengthened basement of the Home Office building in Whitehall.

Similar in design to the Air Ministry War Room at Wealdstone, the Admiralty bunker was constructed beneath the Admiralty Chart Factory at Oxgate Lane in Cricklewood. Building appears to have been completed by the end of 1940.

The War Cabinet War Room, known as PADDOCK, built beneath the Post Office Research Station at Dollis Hill, was commissioned some time before June 1941. Unlike the armed forces war rooms, PADDOCK was surmounted by just a single-storey surface office block. PADDOCK is buried some forty feet below ground with the upper of its two storeys protected by five feet of concrete which includes a 'bomb-burster' layer. Three feet of concrete protected the lower floor.

Above: The surviving surface building of the Admiralty Chart Factory, situated at the junction of Oxgate Lane and Edgeware Road in Cricklewood.
Below: The west end of the flood-prone lower floor spine corridor of the Admiralty Citadel, with the blast door at the bottom of the west staircase visible in the background. The upper floor of the bunker, which lies just above flood level, is currently used as a carpet warehouse.

Above: The upper floor spine corridor at PADDOCK.
Below: The War Cabinet Map Room on the lower floor of PADDOCK. Abandoned at the end of the war, the lower floor soon flooded but was pumped out by Subterranea Britannica, an underground research group, in 2001.

For a number of reasons, including the logistical difficulties involved in transposing large numbers of staff to the suburbs, the effects this might have on morale, and the fact that the expected German aerial onslaught never fully materialised, the northwest London war rooms were soon seen as largely irrelevant encumbrances rather than valuable assets. Instead, it was decided that, in the interim at least, the government departments would remain in Whitehall for as long as possible, protected where necessary by emergency war rooms created in makeshift basement shelters. The most famous of these is the Cabinet War Rooms beneath the former Ministry of Works offices in Great George Street, which is now one of London's prime visitor attractions. The task of reinforcing the overhead cover of the Cabinet War Rooms in October 1940, some months before PADDOCK was completed, indicates that even at that early date the utility of the suburban bunkers was in doubt.

By the autumn of 1940 the Cabinet had made a firm decision that the seat of government would remain in Whitehall. Specifications were issued for the construction of a series of new, hardened war rooms including a citadel for the War Office, known colloquially as 'the Fortress' beneath the now demolished annexe to the former Ministry of Labour offices in Montague House; the monolithic Admiralty citadel on Horse Guards Avenue; protected accommodation for the War Office at Curzon Street House, and a control room for the London Civil Defence Region constructed adjacent to the Geological Museum on Exhibition Road, Kensington.

The Rotundas

A further group of hardened citadels were constructed on the site of the London Gas Light & Coke Company's gasholders on a plot of land bounded by Great Peter Street, Monck Street, Marsham Street and Horseferry Road. These three buildings, two enormous circular structures known as 'the Rotundas', and an adjacent steel-framed building sometimes referred to as 'the Blockhouse', figured largely in the early Cold War plans for safeguarding the machinery of government in war. Although gas production at Horseferry Road ceased in 1875 following the construction of the Gas Light & Coke Company's huge new gasworks at Beckton in East London, the site was occupied by two very large, circular gasholders. These were demolished in 1937, leaving two sixty-foot-deep circular pits on the site. Immediately before the start of the Second World War the gas company made preparation to erect a new headquarters

Above: The visible, upper storey of the south Rotunda, with the Steel Framed Building in the background. The conical structure on the roof of the Rotunda incorporates part of the air-conditioning plant, while the rectangular building constructed partly on a cantilevered platform to the left houses a small auxiliary generating set.

Above: This photograph of the demolition of the Rotundas in 2003 illustrates both the scale of the buildings and the massive thicknesses of concrete incorporated in their structures. *Photo: Bob Jenner.*

building of steel-framed construction on the southern edge of the compound facing Monck Street. Early in 1940 however, before work had proceeded far, the site was requisitioned by the government for the construction of alternative, bomb-proof accommodation for the Air Ministry. Erection of the five-storey steel-framed building went ahead, with the basement and ground floors reinforced as a bomb-proof blockhouse. Meanwhile, in November 1940, the contractors John Mowlem & Company started work on a vast, reinforced concrete bomb-proof circular citadel in the northern gasholder pit while Higgs & Hill Ltd began construction of a similar bunker in the south pit. Both Rotundas consisted of three floors, one-and-a-half of which were completely underground while the above-ground sections were protected by massively thick concrete walls and by roofs formed from no less than twelve feet of reinforced concrete. Construction was largely completed by June 1941 but it appears that the Air Ministry did not take up occupation until early the following year as the communications facilities were not completed until the end of December 1941.

The Horseferry Road complex was built on a lavish scale, with accommodation for a staff of 2,000. It was fully gas-proofed with a sophisticated ventilation and air filtration plant, and had its own secure water supply from an artesian well. The basement of the south Rotunda housed a power station and an extensive communication facility including a thirty-position manual telephone switchboard, teleprinters, radio communications equipment and cypher machines.

Although built primarily for the Air Ministry, the Rotundas and the Blockhouse were home to a rather fluid range of occupants during the progress of the war. In October 1942 the majority of the north Rotunda and the upper floor of the south Rotunda were handed over to the War Office for the use of GHQ Land Forces and 21 Army Group, the Air Ministry contingent previously there retreating to the Blockhouse. Meanwhile, the Ministry of Home Security established its central war room in the north Rotunda. The threat of the German 'V1' flying bombs and, more urgently, of the 'V2' missiles, resulted in the Air Ministry extending its occupancy of the south Rotunda while the basement of the north Rotunda was earmarked for use as a reserve Cabinet War Room. The new Cabinet War Room facility, code-named ANSON, included working, living and sleeping space for Prime Minister Winston Churchill and his wife, the Prime Minister's staff and the War Cabinet. Churchill, it would appear, was as unwilling to use ANSON as he had been PADDOCK earlier in the war and it is probable that ANSON was never fully utilised.

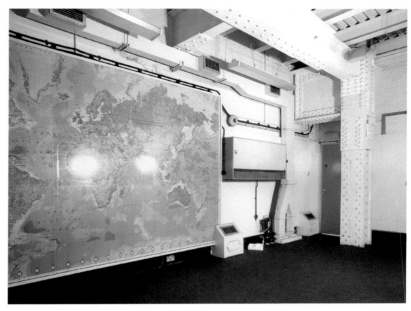

Above: Wall map of the world still in-situ in one of the briefing rooms in the Steel Framed Building, shortly before its demolition.
Below: The distortion seen here in the ceiling and right-hand wall of the tunnel linking the Steel Framed Building to the south Rotunda was the result of a near-miss by a V1 flying bomb towards the end of the Second World War.

By the early 1950s the north Rotunda had been re-equipped to function as the Home Security War Room. In the event of war with the Soviet Union, whether conventional or atomic, the north Rotunda would have acted as a central communications hub for a network of thirteen Regional War Rooms (RWRs) spread throughout the country. At that time it was envisaged that a Soviet attack, even using atomic bombs, would have consequences not much worse than those resulting from the most severe conventional bombing of the Second World War. City centres and military installations, the assumed targets, might be completely destroyed but the majority of the country, and even the suburbs of the larger conurbations, would be relatively unscathed. The RWR concept was based upon the probability that, even if London and the seat of government were not destroyed, there might be severe communications dislocation and contact with the central administration could be restricted or lost for some time. Under these circumstances Regional Commissioners located in the RWRs would assume much of the responsibility for many aspects of central government until communication was restored. Thereafter, general directions to the regions would be issued from the Home Security War Room and information from the regions would be collected

Below: This view of an area known as 'the Crescent', on the lower floor of the south Rotunda, clearly illustrates the curved shape of the bunker's outer wall.

and collated there. The RWRs were, however, seen essentially as little more than sophisticated Civil Defence Control Centres; their principal task was the rescue and recovery of survivors and the co-ordination of essential services, much as had been the role of the Civil Defence Corps during the Second World War. It was expected that in the aftermath of an atomic attack, survivors would be picked from the wreckage of their houses, they would be given a cup of tea, bulldozers would clear the rubble from the streets, men from the water and gas boards would re-connect the pipes and life would resume more-or-less as normal.

As early as 1948 there had been high-level discussions about the machinery of government in wartime and the following year this culminated in a report prepared by a Working Party on the Staffing and Accommodation Plan for the War Cabinet Secretariat. Initially it was expected that the extended Second World War Cabinet War Rooms would be sufficient to house the core of government but it was soon realised that even with the substantial additional overhead cover added in the early post-war years, it was still dangerously vulnerable even to attack using only conventional high-explosive bombs. Following a discussion between Treasury and Ministry of Works officials a scheme, code-named SCOUT, was prepared for the adaption of the now vacant south Rotunda for use as the alternative Cabinet Office War Room. Staffing levels, however, presented insurmountable obstacles as the building could only accommodate around 300 people if sleeping, domestic and catering facilities were to be provided for medium to long periods. A number of other schemes for underground government accommodation in and around Whitehall were also under consideration at this time, including a plan, known as PIRATE, for a series of three parallel, underground tube-type tunnels with lateral linking passages, large enough to accommodate at least a thousand civil servants, burrowing deep beneath Horse Guards Parade. This, like a similar plan for a rather smaller tube-type shelter beneath a proposed new office block in Abingdon Street, intended to house a representative cross section of the House of Commons and House of Lords, was not proceeded with. Some new underground works were completed at that time, including a new bunker for the Air Ministry adjacent to Montague House, known as Whitehall Gardens, and extensions to a wartime tube-type tunnel approximately ninety feet below Whitehall, built by the GPO that carried communications cables between the various war rooms. These GPO tunnels also housed an extensive manual telephone and teleprinter switching centre.

Chapter 2

SUBTERFUGE

Up until the early months of 1951 there was no question that in the event of war government would remain in London until it was absolutely suicidal to continue doing so. There was in this decision both practicality and dogma. If the nucleus of government was to evacuate the capital it would be impotent without its necessarily huge support staff, and to evacuate the whole of Whitehall would be logistically formidable. All the complex national and international communications facilities required by government were concentrated in London as were the foreign embassies, financial institutions and other commercial institutions, interaction with which the smooth running of government depended upon. Parallel with this was the belief that evacuation would be interpreted by the mass of the population, by our foreign allies and by our enemies, as running away, throwing-in the towel and admitting at least the probability of defeat before the fight had begun. By the spring of 1951, however, a new air of realism was in the air. A top secret Cabinet committee had already considered the problem and in April the Cabinet Secretary, Norman Brook, reported its conclusions to Prime Minister Clement Atlee. In the aftermath of a Soviet attack, he reported:

> 'London might become completely isolated and out of touch with the rest of the country; and in that event there would be no object in keeping the central machinery of government underground in London. We are therefore beginning also to consider the possibility of providing some alternative seat of government in another part of the country and equipping it in advance with the necessary accommodation and communications.'

A few months earlier the Cabinet had convened a committee under the chairmanship of a senior Treasury official, Sir Edward Playfair, to develop ideas and report upon proposals for the distribution of government staffs in wartime. In simple terms, the committee's conclusion was that during the lead-up to war approximately 45,000 civil servants should be evacuated to the provinces in a phased process while the majority, some 75,000 in number, should remain in London until the ferocity of attack rendered it impossible for them to reach their place of work, after which they too would be evacuated. A nucleus of 7,800 essential staff would still remain in London working in the various Whitehall citadels until the War Cabinet and other senior staffs were forced to leave. There remained a marked reluctance to abandon London, but a Whitehall-oriented solution presented a serious obstacle in that the available hardened accommodation was insufficient for the number of staff currently envisaged as the minimum that would be required for administration in wartime. Even after a thorough departmental review, completed in May 1952, the Playfair Committee was told that the available accommodation could house little more than half of the proposed 7,800 civil servants. Throughout the early 1950s the PIRATE project was frequently revisited and proposals put forward to extend the existing underground accommodation to provide for the full government manpower requirement. But, taking into account other issues such as the immediate vulnerability of the capital, there was a growing consensus that only a facility far from London would adequately satisfy all the criteria.

In the summer of 1951 Playfair formed a small group of senior civil servants, including Eric de Normann from the Ministry of Works, who had previously been involved in planning a number of underground projects in the West Country during the Second World War. Their task was to consider possible locations for an alternative seat of government outside London. It is probable that de Normann had given thought to this some years earlier for as early as 1946, in reply to one of his subordinate's questions regarding the eventual disposal of the Spring Quarry underground aircraft factory at Corsham, he said of the site that 'the policy is to hold on firmly to our best refuge from the atom bomb.' For a few years after the war the underground telephone exchange in the Bristol Aeroplane Company's factory had become something of a tourist attraction with frequent organised visits arranged for children from various Wiltshire secondary schools. Early in 1947, however, access was suddenly restricted on the grounds that 'the future use of the site might be somewhat sensitive.' It is not surprising, then, that at the meeting in January 1951 de Normann drew to the committee's attention the potential utility of the Corsham quarries.

In a revised report issued in September 1952 the Playfair Committee looked in more detail at the Corsham quarries under cover of a project given the code-name SUBTERFUGE. The underground aircraft engine factory at Spring Quarry, extending over some 3,300,000 square feet, had immediately ceased production at the end of the Second World War. Subsequently, some areas were occupied on a temporary basis by the Ministry of Supply as rough storage accommodation, and over the following few years the Admiralty acquired substantial blocks of underground space there to fulfil its long-term storage requirements. The greater part of the quarry, amounting to approximately 1,970,000 square feet, remained unallocated. The Ministry of Works & Building, de Normann's own department, surveyed the quarry and produced a report sufficiently favourable for the Playfair Committee to request an outline costing for developing an alternative government headquarters there.

Two schemes were proposed, both based upon a nominal population of 12,000 personnel. The first was for what was essentially an austerity scheme that could be implemented within six months. A little less than 1,000,000 square feet of the disused factory would require adaptation and conversion under this scheme to provide working space only; staff would be accommodated in the large hostel and married quarters estates constructed on the surface to house the factory workers. Much of this housing remained empty during the war because workers and their families refused to live in them, compelling the Bristol Aeroplane Company and the Ministry of Transport to arrange for fleets of buses to transport a large proportion of the 12,500 workforce daily between Corsham and the northern suburbs of Bristol. At the time the Playfair Committee was sitting, most of the accommodation was occupied by displaced east European refugees and the government foresaw difficulties in moving them out.

The alternative scheme would require the whole of the 1,970,000 square feet available at Spring Quarry and, in certain iterations, would also have included the three other quarries in north Wiltshire formerly occupied by the Ministry of Aircraft Production at Monk's Park, Westwood near Bradford-on-Avon, and Hayes Wood at Limpley Stoke, which was some eleven miles distant by road. Under this plan, which it was estimated would take two years to complete, the entire workforce would be housed underground, sleeping in bunked dormitories. From its initiation, the proponents of the Spring Quarry SUBTERFUGE scheme stressed that both working and living

conditions would be spartan in nature: 'There should be no illusion,' commented the Playfair Committee report, 'about the standards of working and living conditions which we propose; they will be hard and uncomfortable in the first instance and will never be easy even if our long-term plan is carried out.'

The Padmore Working Party

During 1953 a series of committees and subordinate working parties were set up under the overall control of the newly-formed Cabinet Office Home Defence Committee, chaired by the Cabinet Secretary, Norman Brook, to establish a consistent civil and military response to the threat of a Soviet attack using atomic weapons. As part of this process the Hall Committee had made an assessment of the likely consequences of an attack employing 200 atomic bombs, and the result made for very sombre reading. Hall acknowledged that a robust government was required throughout the transition to war and its aftermath, probably exercising its power from a location outside London, but Padmore's response was that for reasons of morale and international credibility the nucleus of government should still remain in London. By this time the SUBTERFUGE plan was gaining acceptance and those privy to the SUBTERFUGE secret were coming to the conclusion that all the peripheral functions of government should be relocated to Corsham during the build-up to war. In the words of the Padmore Working Party's report issued in November 1953, 'the nucleus Government [which] must include the minimum number of ministers, including the War Cabinet, and officials necessary to control the higher strategy of the war, foreign and commonwealth relations and the major issues of home defence' should continue to function from the London citadels, but 'everybody else must go.'

After this, the situation developed more quickly. Early in 1954 Padmore was asked to review his conclusions in light of the perceived threat from nuclear weapons. The growing awareness of the truly devastating effects of these weapons, with destructive powers potentially a thousand times greater than the existing generation of atomic bombs, required a complete recasting of all the existing home defence assumptions. Clearly London, a key target, would cease to exist under a nuclear onslaught so the London citadels would become irrelevancies. Padmore reversed his original recommendation that the nucleus should remain in London, saying instead that the interests of national morale and international opinion would be better served if the seat of Britain's ultimate authority should evacuate first, even before the first onslaught came, from a capital that would inevitably be reduced to dust and ashes. In this way the continuity of government could be demonstrated to have survived. This proposal met with a surprising volume of opposition and a response verging upon panic. Several ministers and civil servants were insistent that government must remain in London come what may, others cast doubt upon SUBTERFUGE being any safer, while others suggested that government should be fragmented and dispersed into the regions, rather along the lines that were subsequently adopted, more than a decade later, under what was to become known as the PYTHON concept. The Padmore Working Party, however, stuck to its guns, although concessions were made to pacify those who remained committed to the policy of remaining in the London citadels.

Padmore realised that in the aftermath of a nuclear war it would be impossible for government to micro-manage the country in the manner, and using the machinery, that had existed pre-war. Many of its functions would have to be abandoned and many would be irrelevant while others would have to be devolved, perhaps for an extended period, to lower tiers of government in the regions and below. A largely unaddressed aspect of the post-apocalyptic future envisioned by the Padmore Working Party was the fate of around 70,000 Whitehall civil servants for whom there would be no post-war role. One must assume that, like the millions of other workers whose factories and offices had been destroyed, they would simply be set adrift to fend for themselves. Some 5,000 or so might find a role in one of the ten Regional Seats of Government that evolved from the deliberations of the recently convened Cabinet Office Home Defence Committee, and which were seen by Padmore as a vital element in his structure of the machinery of government in war. Indeed, it was a principal element in the larger scheme of things that at the moment that the seat of government evacuated to its emergency headquarters at Corsham the regional government and military headquarters (housed together in a combined, hardened bunker later to be referred to as Regional Seats of Government) should be activated, taking control of the majority of the functions of central government.

It is quite evident that the Padmore team were convinced that the London bunkers would not survive, but, to pacify those whose opinion differed, they suggested that the three Second World War era bunkers in the Harrow area might be earmarked as possible alternative government locations. Writing to the Ministry of Works, Padmore stated that:

'If Ministers accept our recommendation that it should be left to the Government of the day to decide whether the central nucleus should be moved out of London, we are bound to keep accommodation available for it in case the decision be against pre-hostilities evacuation. Indeed if any of the population are expected to stay at work in London, as I understand is contemplated, some element of the government, even if only a suicide squad with no real function to perform in the control structure, would have to remain behind, since the government would clearly have to set an example.

'This I think means that if the citadels are no longer to be retained as bolt-holes for government staffs in war, we have got to find some alternative, not necessarily in central London but in the London area. My understanding is that the Ministry of Works view the combined dangers of shock, flooding and entombment make the citadels an unsuitable choice for anyone who had to stay in London and that other sites, perhaps a little further from the centre, would give at least a slightly better chance of survival.'

More than a year later no firm decision had been made on the future of the London citadels, but the view of de Normann and the Ministry of Works is evident from a letter sent to Sir Thomas Padmore from the Ministry of Works in July 1955:

'… even if government staffs or other people had to stay at work in London they would stand a better chance of survival almost anywhere than in these places. But our report leaves it open to the Government of the day to decide whether or not to leave London. So long therefore as the possibility of the central nucleus remaining (however unlikely we believe that contingency to be) we must presumably hold accommodation available for them.'

With momentum now driving the concept of an emergency government headquarters outside London, the Home Defence Committee now proposed not one but two alternative bolt-holes. The reasoning behind this decision was based upon two imperatives, the most important being the conclusions of a committee set up under the chairmanship of a treasury official William Strath towards the end of 1954 to investigate the structural and economic consequences of the effects of radioactive fallout, which had previously not been considered. The report of the Strath Committee, issued in March 1955, was shocking, revelatory and completely altered the direction of the plans for the continuity of government in war. Strath predicted apocalyptic devastation with some 16,000,000 dead and millions more sick and injured with little hope of recovery, half the country virtually obliterated and at least forty percent of its industrial capacity destroyed. Nuclear radiation would make movement in the open impossible for days or weeks after the initial attack and might render some areas permanently unapproachable. It was now realised that the next world war would not be like those before, even though planning to date had been based upon previous experience. The injured would not be picked from the wreckage and given succour, Londoners would not 'take it' with a cheery grin and a cup of tea. Nor would it be a prolonged war of attrition in the conventional sense. Instead of dragging on for months or dreary years, it would be over, quite literally, in a flash. When it was over the situation would not be, as it was in 1945, that just a few percent of Britain's productive capacity was impaired, her railways and distribution services run-down but serviceable and her vital utilities intact, ready for a post-war building and manufacturing boom. Government's job would not be to manipulate the grand strategy of war, marshal the nation's industrial capacity to feed the war machine, negotiate overseas alliances to its own advantage or nurture the population through periods of temporary shortage. Instead there would be nothing. The only task for government would be to oversee a long, slow period of gradual recovery that might take years or even decades to show fruit.

What now required consideration was what role SUBTERFUGE, or its alternative, was to play. It was assumed that there would be a prolonged period of international tension, probably six months or more, leading up to war. This was the period that caused the planners so much anxiety because they could not decide whether government should continue from London throughout the entire period (for the reasons outlined above), whether the nucleus should evacuate on the eve of war, or wait until the onslaught had begun before decamping to Corsham or wherever else had been selected. As we have seen, to evacuate the whole Whitehall campus was logistically impossible, but it was, at this relatively early stage in the planning process, thought essential that a representative section of each government department should be provided with a haven of safety. This administrative unit could take up residence in their alternative location during the precautionary period gradually taking the reins of their departments, thus relieving pressure on Whitehall staff who perhaps had more pressing war-orientated tasks to oversee, and assume full control if or when the London contingent ceased to exist.

The central nucleus posed the greater problem, for was it to display weakness and decamp to Corsham during the late precautionary phase or was it to sit in London until it was suicidal to remain? An option was to create a secondary nucleus of higher ranking ministers who would go down to Corsham (or possibly to the alternative location) and prepare to assume ultimate control if the Prime Minister and the War Cabinet, who would stay in London until the very last moment, failed to make it to Corsham. This dilemma raised the question of whether or not SUBTERFUGE would have or require any war-making function. If it were manned by the central nucleus before the outbreak of hostilities, or if control was assumed by a 'second-eleven' of ministers because the principal nucleus had been destroyed before it could evacuate and before it could authorise nuclear retaliation, then SUBTERFUGE would become an alternative location for the authorisation of nuclear retaliation, with all the ramifications that such a course of action would entail. The main task of the survivor government, however, would be to oversee a prolonged, austere period of survival and slow recovery.

Probably influenced by de Normann, the Padmore Working Party proposed the former underground aircraft engine component factory at Drakelow, near Kidderminster, as the location for the second alternative emergency government war headquarters. Previously, as we have seen, three other quarries in north Wiltshire had been identified as expansion locations for SUBTERFUGE; all were developed for the Ministry of Aircraft Production as underground factories on behalf of de Normann's department, the Ministry of Works. Similarly, the Ministry of Works was also the progenitor of the Drakelow factory, and also of another underground factory at Warren Row near Maidenhead, which was earmarked at an early stage for conversion to a regional seat of government. Over the next three years the Drakelow site, code-named MACADAM, was much debated but, as we shall see, these plans, as far as a central government role was concerned, came to nothing. Work on MACADAM was not scheduled to begin until SUBTERFUGE was completed, and by that time every aspect of the emergency government plans had undergone radical overhaul.

SUBTERFUGE *proposals become reality*

SUBTERFUGE limped into life in February 1954 without Treasury or Ministerial approval. The first indication of its birth appeared in a letter from the Ministry of Works to the Treasury requesting preliminary funding of £100,000 to begin construction:
'We hope to spend this money on the initial stages of a scheme known as SUBTERFUGE about which we have been forbidden to say

anything on paper if we can possibly avoid it. However, Padmore knows about the scheme and perhaps the simplest course would be for you to refer to him.

'We are in rather an awkward position about this scheme because although we have received authority to put £100,000 in the Estimates, we have not yet received Treasury authority for the scheme as a whole nor indeed have we got Ministerial authority as yet. The project is included in an interim report recently submitted by Padmore's Working Party to the Home Defence Committee. The cost of the whole scheme was estimated some little time ago at about £1,000,000 although it may well reach £1,250,000 before it is finished, which should take about three years.'

The immediate Treasury response was:

'Seems putting the cart before the horse; shouldn't we await Ministerial approval before giving them Treasury approval (which means nothing so far as the details are concerned, as we have yet been told nothing about methods of construction, etc.)?'

The Ministry of Works endeavoured to explain the urgency and importance of the scheme without giving away any of its essential secrets, prefacing a costed list of preliminary works they intended to do with the comment: 'as to what we want to do as distinct from where we want to do it, we propose to spend the £100,000 as follows …'

The list includes a number of items that are difficult to explain because it implies a requirement for expenditure on facilities, particularly sewerage and water supply facilities, which already existed on site and which still survive today in much the same condition. There is, for example, a reference to £30,000 required for reservoirs and an emergency sewage pipeline, both of which were provided, at very great expense, to serve the Ministry of Aircraft Production factory in 1942. New boreholes were sunk in the Chippenham area to tap additional water supplies, new pipelines were laid and reservoirs constructed at Corsham to provide sufficient supplies not only for the underground factory but also for the domestic accommodation built for the 25,000 men and women who worked in the factory. Another compound item on the list, costing £58,000, included the provision of lavatories underground (all of which, in fact, already existed and required virtually no extra work or expenditure), the construction of a concrete ring wall to enclose the protected area, and the provision of canteen equipment. Not only was much of the proposed work unnecessary, but the costings for those items that were required bore little similarity to the actual costs. The concrete ring wall, for

example, along with a few other items of builders' work, was just a few months later estimated at £400,000. Before looking further at the construction of SUBTERFUGE, it is perhaps worth studying what existed below and above ground at Corsham in order to understand the magnitude of the task faced by the Home Defence Committee and the Ministry of Works.

As we have seen, Spring Quarry at Corsham, the location earmarked as the site of the proposed Central Government War Headquarters, was a former Bath stone quarry converted during the Second World War into an underground factory for the use of Bristol Aeroplane Company. 3,300,000 square feet of quarry space was allocated to the factory but approximately one third of this, comprising the northwest quadrant, was never developed although it is contained within the factory's secure perimeter. Of what remained, the southwest section, which had been occupied during the war by the Birmingham Small Arms Company, was handed over to the Admiralty for storage, a function that continued up until the mid-1990s. A small area to the southeast was used briefly by the Ministry of Supply for rough storage but the rest, comprising the whole of the central and northern sections of the eastern end of the quarry remained unoccupied under a tacit agreement with the Cabinet Office. Within this area all the machine tools had been removed, many of them having been American Lend-Lease machines which immediately reverted to US ownership when the conflict ended. The only evidence of their previous existence was a plethora of concrete bases and holdfast bolts, and extensive patches of lubricant and coolant that had seeped into the surrounding floor. The existing 11kV electrical distribution system, including thirty-four three-phase sub-stations providing a total of 17 Megawatts at 440 volts, remained intact, along with a comprehensive single-phase 240 volt lighting and power system. The factory's ventilation and air heating and distribution system also survived intact, the induction and circulating fans, for the most part, remaining in use until the site was decommissioned in 2004. Treated air was circulated by means of extensive under-floor ducts and a floor-to-ceiling airway that encompassed the northern and eastern extremity of the quarry. Major changes were, however, made to the air distribution system during the development of SUBTERFUGE, and the heating system was later abandoned. Steam for the original heating system, and for factory process purposes, was provided by a boilerhouse at the west end of the site containing six coal-fired boilers. These were augmented by a further six boilers located in a second underground installation in the BSA section of the quarry. The latter were converted to oil-firing in the early 1960s to power heater batteries in the Admiralty storage depot. In the area earmarked for SUBTERFUGE only two boilers were retained and were subsequently converted to oil-firing, the space previously occupied by the other four being later used to accommodate four diesel generator sets. The retained boilers initially provided steam for cooking appliances in the two underground kitchens and to provide hot water in the ablution areas by means of heat exchangers or calorifiers. In the mid-1970s all the underground boilers were decommissioned and their function taken over by a new boilerhouse on the surface, readily identified by its distinctive quatrefoil chimney stack. Thirty-one extensive ablution blocks including male and female toilets, washing facilities and a more modest number of showers survived the factory era, the majority of which were ultimately incorporated into SUBTERFUGE with little or no modification.

Access to the SUBTERFUGE area was via the two Otis escalators already referred to, which were still operational in the late 1950s, and via two passengers lifts (PL1 and PL2), goods lift GL1 and an open, vertical shaft with a winch over, used as a machinery lift and known as ML1. There was also a pedestrian stairway in the original Spring Quarry slope shaft at the east end of the quarry and underground connections with the adjoining War Office and Air Ministry quarries to the north and with the Admiralty areas to the south and west.

The sections of the former factory to be developed as SUBTERFUGE consisted of the whole area north of the main east-west road, northwards to the War Office boundary, machine shops one to six inclusive, the tool, general and raw materials stores to the west of the machine shops and the extensive service area to the east. The machine shops were predominantly open areas each approximately five acres in extent interspersed with a random arrangement of roof support pillars while the services areas were generally sub-divided into smaller rooms by brick or concrete block walls. The general layout of the factory roadways was retained to serve the SUBTERFUGE project; most of the building work required consisted of the levelling of floors and the erection of new partition walls to provide the necessary office space.

Work begins

Despite the earlier Treasury misgivings, Prime-Ministerial authority was eventually granted in September 1955 for the construction of SUBTERFUGE at an estimated cost of £1,200,000, exclusive of the cost of office, catering and domestic equipment. Of this, £400,000 was earmarked for infrastructure work including the construction underground of a six-foot-thick concrete perimeter wall, additional concrete reinforcements to the head-works of the existing lifts and escalators, blast-proofing the tops of the existing ventilation shafts, building internal partition walls and levelling floors, and constructing a large underground water reservoir. The remaining £800,000 would be absorbed by the installation of new air-conditioning plant and heat exchangers, the provision of four standby generator sets and a water treatment plant, upgrading the existing 11kV electricity distribution system and renovation of the wartime sewage disposal plant, ventilation fans and compressed air plant. Major modifications were also required to the boilerhouse, including, as we have seen, the removal of four of the six existing coal-fired boilers and conversion of the remaining pair to oil-firing. A note prepared by the Ministry of Works, dated January 1956, made the point that 'no provision is made for office and canteen equipment, which might amount to £50 per head of staff (say £40 for office and £7 for canteen equipment), or an additional £200,000 on the basis of a staff of 4,000.

After a prolonged period of frustrating negotiation with the various government departments, the Padmore Working Party arrived at a manning level and an organisational structure that would both satisfy the functional requirements of SUBTERFUGE and fit comfortably within the space available. By May 1956 it was established that SUBTERFUGE would accommodate a staff of 4,000 of whom 1,000 would be senior decision makers and of whom one quarter would be female. Of the remaining 3,000 personnel, a little more than 1,200 would be involved with communications while the majority of the rest would consist of clerical staff along with a relatively small contingent of guards and site management and maintenance staff.

Once the functions and manning levels were agreed, detailed plans were prepared for the physical layout of SUBTERFUGE, including the arrangement and types of office, catering and domestic space that would be provided. Plans for sleeping accommodation were also drawn up; these facilities included double-duty offices that served as individual offices and bedrooms for some 250 senior staff and bunked dormitories for the lower orders. The whole complex was grouped around a War Cabinet Map Room, overlooked by an adjacent conference room. This was located centrally in what was during the factory era known as 'the deep area', a high-ceilinged section of the quarry in which engine assembly was completed. Those departments most directly concerned with the prosecution of the war and contending with its aftermath were in closest proximity to the Cabinet War Room; the Foreign and Commonwealth Office and its associated communications centre were situated to the south, the Ministries of Power and Transport, both vital to post-war recovery, were to the immediate north. The more distant areas were occupied by the so-called 'due functioning' departments such as the Board of Trade, the Treasury and Inland Revenue, which would have minimal roles to play in the survival period.

A contract for the majority of the groundwork and heavy construction was let to Chivers, a Devizes-based building firm, in July 1956 and within eighteen months most of the work was completed. By that time the site had a secure perimeter, a working ventilation system, toilets, adequate water and electricity supplies, an external sewerage system and an internal emergency sewage treatment plant. Responding to a Cabinet Office enquiry as to whether or not the quarry in its current state could be made operational in an emergency, it was stated that 'measures necessary for the activation of the headquarters would have to be improvised but doubtless the headquarters would be manned after a fashion within seven days.' The principal act of improvisation that would be required was the refurbishment and modification of the existing underground Hawthorn GPO telephone exchange in Area No.1 which had been commissioned in 1942 but had been disused since 1948. Equipment currently installed there included a 500-line automatic exchange, established to provide connections throughout the wartime military and industrial complex in the Neston area, a four-position manual switchboard and a twelve-position manual trunk exchange switchboard. The installation of SUBTERFUGE's dedicated telephone exchange had not yet started and would not be completed until the summer of 1962.

A preliminary operational plan for SUBTERFUGE was issued in January 1958, when it was still assumed that both SUBTERFUGE and the alternative headquarters at Drakelow, code-named MACADAM, would be completed and operated in tandem. The plan proposed that:

'Two self-contained places outside London will be prepared as alternative government war headquarters. These are known as SUBTERFUGE and MACADAM. Both places will be fully manned, including standby teams of Ministers, at the outset of the precautionary period and provision will be made for the reception of the Prime Minister, the War Cabinet, the Chiefs of Staff and

their immediate retinues should the government decide at a later stage to leave London.

'If the government so decides to leave London it will move to SUBTERFUGE unless that place has already been put out of action in which case the government will go to MACADAM. If control from London should become inoperative before the government moves, control will be exercised from SUBTERFUGE so long as it remains in action, failing which it will be exercised from MACADAM. Should London and both alternative headquarters be put out of action national control will be assumed by surviving Regional Headquarters in a prescribed order.'

In the event of the above action becoming necessary, the Cabinet Secretary would invite the Prime Minister to nominate two teams of Ministers to proceed immediately to the two alternative headquarters. Meanwhile, treasury officials privy to the SUBTERFUGE secret would advise the heads of other government departments to implement pre-arranged plans for the movement of designated staff to both alternative war headquarters. Simultaneously, Foreign Office staff would advise diplomatic missions and High Commissioners in this country to implement plans for the evacuation of their own designated staffs to the alternative headquarters.

That was the theory. However, in practice the plan acknowledged that no consideration had been given to the preparation of MACADAM, and that the efficient functioning of SUBTERFUGE would be predominantly determined by the extent of the communications available which, as we have seen, were currently inadequate. Using the facilities available in the wartime exchange only 500 of the required 1,500 internal extensions were available and only twenty-two of the proposed 500 inland telephone circuits. Similarly, just twenty-two out of a required 140 inland telegraph circuits were available and only two out of thirty-five overseas telegraph circuits. With six months' notice, the planners expected that a further thirty-seven inland telephone circuits , twenty-four inland telegraph circuits and seventeen overseas telegraph circuits could be provided, but only at an additional capital cost of £150,000.

A report circulated in June 1959 noted that approximately sixty-five percent of the work was now completed. The main tasks remaining were the installation of the four Mirrlees generators and of two pairs of Sulzer air-conditioning units, one pair to serve the east and one the west end of the headquarters. All were operational by the winter of 1961. By the following August all construction work was complete and supplies of stationery, furniture and reserves of

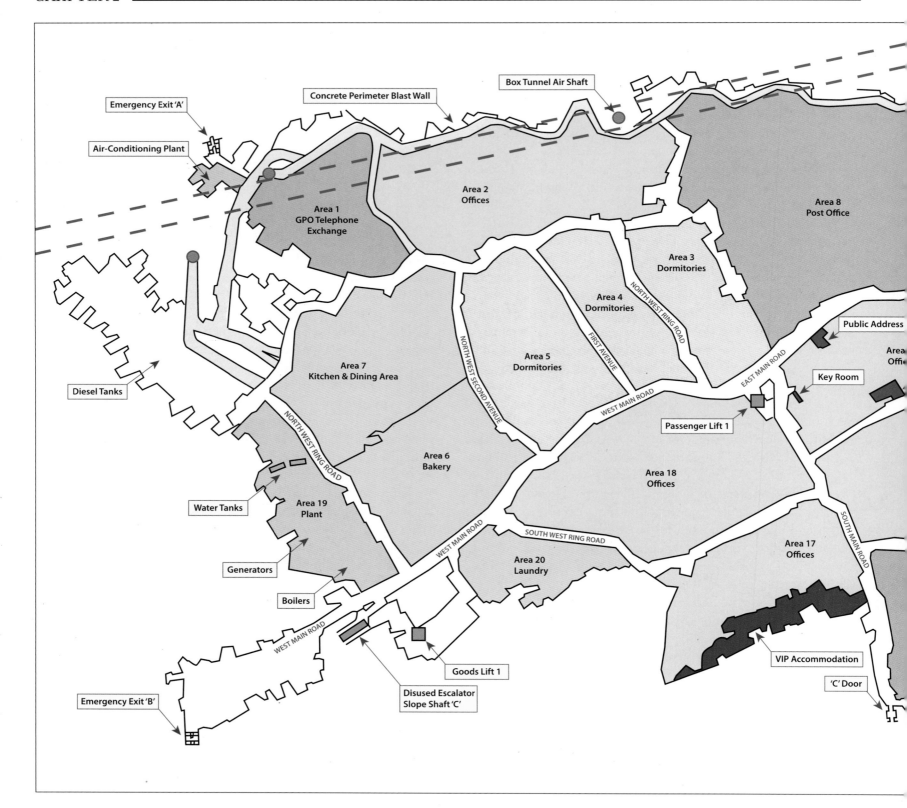

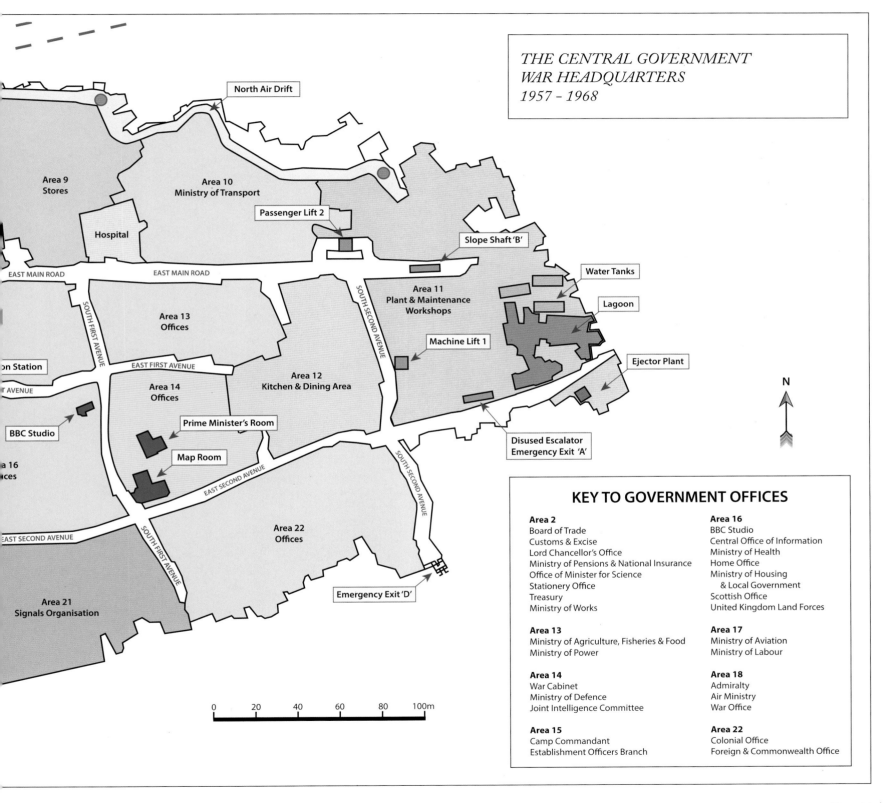

THE CENTRAL GOVERNMENT
WAR HEADQUARTERS
1957 – 1968

North Air Drift

Area 9
Stores

Area 10
Ministry of Transport

Passenger Lift 2

Slope Shaft 'B'

Hospital

Water Tanks

Lagoon

EAST MAIN ROAD

EAST MAIN ROAD

Area 11
Plant & Maintenance
Workshops

Area 13
Offices

Machine Lift 1

Ejector Plant

on Station

EAST FIRST AVENUE

Area 12
Kitchen & Dining Area

AVENUE

Area 14
Offices

BBC Studio

Prime Minister's Room

Disused Escalator
Emergency Exit 'A'

a 16
ces

Map Room

EAST SECOND AVENUE

EAST SECOND AVENUE

Area 22
Offices

KEY TO GOVERNMENT OFFICES

Emergency Exit 'D'

Area 2
Board of Trade
Customs & Excise
Lord Chancellor's Office
Ministry of Pensions & National Insurance
Office of Minister for Science
Stationery Office
Treasury
Ministry of Works

Area 16
BBC Studio
Central Office of Information
Ministry of Health
Home Office
Ministry of Housing
 & Local Government
Scottish Office
United Kingdom Land Forces

Area 13
Ministry of Agriculture, Fisheries & Food
Ministry of Power

Area 17
Ministry of Aviation
Ministry of Labour

Area 21
Signals Organisation

Area 14
War Cabinet
Ministry of Defence
Joint Intelligence Committee

Area 18
Admiralty
Air Ministry
War Office

0   20   40   60   80   100m

Area 15
Camp Commandant
Establishment Officers Branch

Area 22
Colonial Office
Foreign & Commonwealth Office

N

The images on this page are progress photographs taken by the Devizes building firm of W.E. Chivers Ltd in 1959 and show conversion work under way during the development of the CGWHQ at Corsham. Chivers was the prime contractor at Corsham and had a good track record with government projects including work on the Harwell atomic research establishment, the chemical and biological warfare research establishment at Porton Down and many other military building projects on Salisbury Plain. The company also built hospitals, telephone exchanges and schools, and was also responsible for building most of the Second World War pillboxes on the West Country invasion defence lines. These photographs, of what was the nation's most secret and sensitive site, were, however, taken without authority but survived unnoticed in the firm's archive until the company entered receivership in October 1985. The photographs, still unnoticed amongst the rest of the Chivers records, were transferred to Wiltshire County Archives where they were eventually discovered, still uncataloged, by a researcher in 1999.

Above: This photograph shows the reconstruction of the surface head-works of the west escalator. The partially demolished remains of the Second World War building can be seen inside foundations of the massive new, atom-bomb-proof structure. In the right background can be seen the surface building for goods lift GL1 while to the left can be seen the tapering chimney stack of the underground boilerhouse with a condense tank attached to its side.

Below: A view of East Main Road during conversion. There is already indication of some new brickwork, and much of the cabling suspended from the roof appears to be recent. Notice the contractor's battery electric trucks and charging apparatus. This view should be compared with the contemporary photograph of the same scene seen in the frontispiece to this book.

food were arriving. In the early summer of 1963 the Prime Minister was informed that SUBTERFUGE was ready for action if required. The final cost, at £2,500,000 was exactly double the original estimate.

Into action

The code-name of the Corsham headquarters was changed from SUBTERFUGE to STOCKWELL on 25 January 1959. Informed of this change, those privy to the secret were warned that: 'The project is 'Secret'. The code-word is 'Classified' unless used in a context which reveals or implies the purpose and location of the project, in which case the document or conversation in which it is so used becomes 'Top Secret'.'

Exactly what function STOCKWELL would have during the various stages preceding, during, and in the aftermath of a nuclear exchange was a matter of continued debate and, indeed, the status of the site appears to have been in a state of constant flux. A circular letter from the Treasury (whose task when the time came was, as we have seen above, to put other government departments on warning of the imminent move to STOCKWELL), to the various departmental Establishment Officers, outlined the current policy:

'As you know, STOCKWELL is intended primarily as a battle headquarters for the higher direction of the country's administration during the attack and survival periods, and planning to date has been based on this concept. However, on 3 February 1961 the Machinery of Government Sub-Committee agreed that it was desirable to consider what functions STOCKWELL might exercise in the precautionary period before attack. The extent to which the headquarters could take on responsibilities at such a time may affect organisational arrangements in Whitehall and elsewhere. It may also be relevant to the phasing of plans for the manning of STOCKWELL in an emergency; though in view of the importance of ensuring continuance of government control the exercise of functions in the precautionary period could not be allowed to hinder the manning of STOCKWELL very early in the precautionary period if Ministers so ordered.

'It can be argued that STOCKWELL should take over as many functions as possible in the precautionary period. The resultant knowledge of the state of war preparations and the experience gained in operating from the headquarters would ease the task of taking over wholly from Whitehall when the attack came; it would serve as a precaution against a sudden destruction of Whitehall

or the depletion of staff there as a result of evacuation, and of manning regional and other headquarters; and it would make good use of the staff at STOCKWELL at a time when administrative resources would be fully stretched.'

Implicit in this analysis was the assumption that in the precautionary stage most government departments would continue to function much as they had done in peacetime, with their staffs split geographically between Whitehall and STOCKWELL. That certain difficulties would arise from the division of responsibilities between the two locations was foreseen, and it was understood that, without scope for physical expansion, the volume of work for which STOCKWELL could take responsibility was limited. Reflecting upon this, the final paragraph of the letter to Establishment Officers makes the point that:

'In any event STOCKWELL could not deal with the mass of routine work, and during the precautionary period it would probably need support from peacetime offices to implement its decisions. Communications from STOCKWELL might be limited, but all parts of the government organisation would need to be kept informed of what each was doing.'

In May 1961 a revised scheme was prepared for the activation of STOCKWELL. The plan assumed that, as detailed above, there would be a period of international tension before any nuclear attack took place, and that there would be adequate time to prepare and man STOCKWELL. However, if this expectation was not realised then:

'No plans have yet been made to ensure the continuance of government if Whitehall should be destroyed by a surprise attack before government left London. There is not a great deal that could be done in advance to guard against this situation, but it may be worth considering whether Regional Defence Directors should be given instructions to try to make contact with any surviving Ministers and to rally any other staff to Regional Headquarters after attack.'

If the conflict evolved as predicted, an advance contingent would man STOCKWELL in the early precautionary stage and then the following scenario outlined in a secret memorandum entitled The Machinery of Government in War: Ministerial Arrangements would apply:

'Provision has been made at STOCKWELL for the accommodation in the War Cabinet area of the Prime Minister and five other Ministers. It is assumed that the Prime Minister would take over the functions of Minister of Defence in war, but the composition of the War Cabinet has not been considered. The Prime Minister, with a small party of senior Ministers and official and Service advisors, might wish to remain in London for as long as possible in the precautionary period. Special provision has been made for the removal of about twenty-five people to STOCKWELL at short notice in the precautionary stage, but there can be no certainty that these arrangements would be successful.

'Besides the War Cabinet organisation, STOCKWELL is planned to comprise a Home Defence block and representatives of overseas departments, the Service departments and 'due-functioning' home departments. It is assumed that such of these Ministers as are not in the Prime Minister's party would take up their posts at STOCKWELL with the main contingent of staff, when the Cabinet gave the order to man the headquarters. The current study of STOCKWELL's functions in the precautionary period may, however, to some extent affect this assumption. Separate consideration is being given to the possible need to send a senior Minister to STOCKWELL in the early precautionary period to carry out the planned nuclear retaliation procedures if for some reason the Prime Minister is unable to do so. This Minister, who might perhaps be the Home Secretary, might be required to take over from the Prime Minister if the latter fails to reach STOCKWELL before attack.'

The birth of BURLINGTON

By August 1961 (by which time the headquarters had undergone another change of name and was now known as BURLINGTON) a more robust scheme for a reserve government-in-waiting to be put in place at Corsham during the precautionary phase, to take over the reins of government should the Cabinet be wiped out before it could leave the capital, had been developed. Documents from this period stress, however, that BURLINGTON's primary role was a post-attack one:

'The central nucleus of government will remain in London throughout the precautionary period, the function of BURLINGTON will be to act as the seat of government in the period of survival and reconstruction so that while, therefore, the staffs at BURLINGTON will need to be kept currently informed from Whitehall of the progress of war preparatory matter (so that they can take over smoothly when and if necessary) no substantive functions will be exercised from BURLINGTON during the precautionary stage.'

The only situation in which BURLINGTON would exercise anything other than a 'survival and recovery' role would be if the nucleus of government was either destroyed or its means of communication incapacitated by enemy action before it had been able to authorise retaliation. The question of the legal competence of the reserve body at BURLINGTON to take such executive action was raised in correspondence between the Cabinet Office and the Treasury Solicitor, in which the latter noted that:

'I understand that the idea now is that a kind of 'second-eleven' of Ministers will be going to BURLINGTON at the precautionary stage. If they have to take over the Central Government the situation will not be such as to make legal forms of great importance, but nevertheless our purpose is to clothe them with legal and constitutional authority. They will need to exercise emergency powers under defence Regulations, etc., and also prerogative powers. As regards emergency powers which are given to a particular Minister, for example the Secretary of State for War, the powers would be exercisable in his name as long as he exists, but would cease if there were no Secretary of State for War. As regards prerogative powers, which derive directly from the Sovereign, it is necessary that a Minister purporting to exercise them should have authority from the Queen.'

In the summer of 1997 the investigative reporter Duncan Campbell discovered a document in the National Archives that had slipped through the Cabinet Office security net and which gave the first concrete evidence of the existence of the Corsham bunker, (which had long been supposed), and of its function in the event of nuclear war. This document, a top secret report from the Emergency Government War Headquarters Inter Services Committee, or EGWISC, chaired by G.R.D. Fitzpatrick, was the first to show the code-name BURLINGTON in use, and it is very much on account of this that the name, although used only for a few months, has become the one with which the Corsham headquarters is immediately associated. An annexe to the main report detailed the various departments that would be represented at BURLINGTON together with their manning requirements. The Cabinet Organisation, the document explained, would:

'... act as the ultimate source of authority during the period of survival and reconstruction, and be an alternative centre to London for authorising Nuclear Retaliation. It is assumed that the Prime Minister would take on the responsibility for defence and that the War Cabinet would consist of a small number of senior Ministers with other Ministers and Chiefs of Staff attending meetings as required. The Chiefs of Defence Staff would be housed in the War Cabinet Organisation area, but other Chiefs of Staff would be elsewhere in the headquarters. The War Cabinet Organisation would include a number of supporting staffs, e.g. Secretariats (civil and military) Intelligence and Map Room staffs, Ministry of Defence representatives and common services such as registry and typing.'

A senior staff of sixty-three military personnel was included in the Cabinet Organisation, including the Chief of the Defence Staff, the Chiefs of Staff Secretariat, the Joint Planning Staff, and the staff from the Prime Minister's Map Room. The document went on to outline the functions of the various civil and military departments in some detail, a few examples of which are listed below.

The task of the Admiralty contingent was:

- To provide the government with professional naval advice that will enable it to intervene effectively to influence the conduct of war at sea where the national interest requires.

The functions of the Home Office were:

- To oversee overall policy for the maintenance and restoration of law and order.
- To advise the Army Council and Chiefs of Staff and implement their directives.
- To provide members of Joint Services Committees.
- To redeploy manpower and logistic resources between commands.
- To prepare the country for survival and recovery.

Aware that the resources of the police might quickly be over-extended, it was noted that 'the implementation of certain of the functions will be delegated to the United Kingdom Land Forces. UKLF, in turn, was warned that its role would be absolutely subservient to the civil authority of the Home Office.

The role of the Air Ministry, which at this time had not yet handed control of the nuclear deterrent to the Royal Navy, was:

- To operate nuclear retaliation, or those aspects of nuclear retaliation that remain to be completed.
- To provide liaison in connection with, and logistic support of, those elements of the RAF which are or will be assigned to SACEUR and SACLANT.
- To control global RAF activity, in particular operation of the air transport forces.
- To contribute support, both in manpower and logistically in joint action during the survival phase.
- To liaise with any surviving USAF in the United Kingdom.

When the time came for the nucleus of government to leave London,

the small party of VIPs would leave Horse Guards Parade aboard a helicopter bound for Corsham. Included in the helicopter party would be:

- The Prime Minister and his immediate advisors.
- Chief of the Defence Staff.
- Secretary to the Chiefs of Staff Committee.
- The First Sea Lord, his Secretary and Naval Assistant.
- Chief of the Imperial General Staff and two advisors.
- Chief of the Air Staff and two immediate advisors.

Previously, the rest of the military contingent, five senior ministers and those government civil servants who were allocated desks at BURLINGTON, would have travelled to the West Country in a series of special trains from Kensington Olympia station, to which they would have been taken by a fleet of requisitioned buses that had collected them from a number of discreet, pre-allocated pickup points near their peacetime places of work. The trains would take them not directly to Corsham but to Warminster station, some thirty miles away. From there they would be taken by army transport to the nearby School of Infantry, code-named CHECK POINT, from where, at a suitable time they would be transported as surreptitiously as possible, in small numbers to BURLINGTON.

First & second Gravediggers

The consequences of a surprise nuclear attack wiping out the executive nucleus of the British government before it had either reached the safety of BURLINGTON or released a retaliatory nuclear attack in a final act of suicidal folly from its self-imposed Whitehall tomb was a problem that vexed the planners throughout the period of the Cold War when the 'Tripwire' policy of Mutually Assured Destruction was at its zenith. During the autumn of 1961 the Macmillan government gestated a scheme which it hoped offered the solution to this hitherto intractable difficulty. The plan required the consent of two subordinate ministers to whom would be delegated the authority for nuclear release if the Prime Minister, for whatever reason, was unable to issue the instruction himself. A minute from Macmillan dated 13 October 1961 revealed the names of the chosen ministers. In the minute, the Prime Minister commented:

> 'About the nomination of deputies for authorising nuclear retaliation; I agree the following:
> First Gravedigger, Mr R.A. Butler, Second Gravedigger
> Mr Selwyn Lloyd'

A year later, on 26 September 1962, Selwyn Lloyd was replaced by Sir Alex Douglas Home, and his letter of nomination explains the rationale behind his appointment and the role he was to play:

'I have been considering what arrangements should be made to ensure that in time of grave international tension political authority, on behalf of the government, will always be immediately available for the purposes of nuclear retaliation if this should be required.

'The decision to launch nuclear weapons is one of such gravity that it should clearly be taken by Ministers, or by the Prime Minister on behalf of the government, if it is humanly possible to arrange this. But it is the essence of the strategic deterrent that it will be launched without fail if an enemy should attack us first with nuclear weapons, and modern developments have made it possible that the first warning of attack may be received only a few minutes before missiles land.

'Current arrangements provide that if a nuclear attack is delivered, or is known to have been launched, I am to be consulted immediately; but if this proves impossible the competent military authority, if he is certain that an attack has in fact been made, has authority to order nuclear retaliation in the last resort without ministerial authority. This is the only practicable arrangement in the event of a nuclear attack on this country in what would otherwise be normal conditions of peace – in other words a 'bolt from the blue'. But a 'bolt from the blue' which implies the failure of the deterrent policy, and would clearly require immediate retaliation, is unlikely.

'A more likely situation would arise from an increase in international tension to the point where the government would decide to institute the Precautionary Stage. At that stage it would be my duty (except for exceptional purposes such as international negotiations) to remain in London and to be immediately accessible myself at all times, as far as this is physically possible; and I should be in close touch with the President of the United States, with our other allies and with military commanders of NATO and of our own Services. Nevertheless, there would almost certainly be some occasions when I could not be reached for immediate consultation, for instance if I were moving by car from one place to another; and I propose to nominate a Minister to act as my First Deputy, in London, for this purpose at such times.

'There is also the possibility that London might be silenced before the necessary consultations could take place. I propose, therefore, to nominate another Minister as my Second Deputy from amongst those who would go to the alternative headquarters of the central government.

'It will be necessary for the First Deputy to be available to assume responsibility during any period, however short, when I am necessarily out of touch with my main communications. The Second Deputy will be housed at the alternative headquarters of the central government and will have no Parliamentary or other duties which will require him to move away from his communications there. He will be in continuous touch with developments in London and will know immediately if contact is broken that he has necessarily assumed responsibility.'

MACADAM revisited & renamed

Initially, as we have seen, it was proposed that both Spring Quarry and the Drakelow factory site, at first code-named MACADAM but later renamed QUADRANGLE, would be functionally similar and, as far as possible, physical duplicates of one another. At a meeting in November 1958 of the Machinery of Government in War, (MGW), Sub-Committee of Norman Brook's Home Defence Committee it was decided, however, that the second reserve seat of government should not be a duplicate of SUBTERFUGE, then under construction, but should instead, at most, be a 'reserve of experience and authority'. It was subsequently decided that whilst the possible future utility

Below: Typical office accommodation in the Drakelow RSG following the bunker's refurbishment in the 1980s.

Above: The remains of the 1960s BBC studio at Drakelow. There was much vacant space at the site, so a completely new BBC complex was constructed during the 1980s refit and the old studio and control room simply abandoned. *Below:* Similarly, completely new cooking and dining facilities were provided in the 1980s. The early RSG kitchen, which re-used the wartime factory cookhouse, was abandoned and left to decay.

of QUADRANGLE as a reserve seat of central government should not be dismissed, no further action should be taken at present. Instead, a parallel scheme to adapt parts of the underground facility at Drakelow into a regional seat of government was authorised, under the proviso that this would not prejudice the use of the remaining accommodation there by central government if the need arose. Upon this point the MGW Planning Team satisfied themselves that the Regional Headquarters scheme, which would require space for a staff of 450, would leave sufficient accommodation available for a central government contingent of 1,500 personnel.

SUBTERFUGE *in doubt*

No sooner was construction of SUBTERFUGE under way than serious doubts were raised concerning the overall viability of the site, some members of the MGW Sub-Committee voicing the opinion that, essentially, they had lumbered themselves with a white-elephant that could not be kept secret, that did not offer sufficient protection from nuclear weapons and that, giving the planning assumptions that led to its construction, could not, with any degree of reliability, be adequately manned in order to perform its required functions. The problem was that although it was located more than one hundred miles from London and was deep underground, it was neither deep enough nor sufficiently well protected to withstand the effects of even a near miss from a nuclear weapon. SUBTERFUGE relied for its security solely upon the facts that it was remote and that only a handful of people were aware of its location. It was clearly understood from the outset that as soon as information about its location leaked out it would be rendered instantly useless, and it was equally clearly comprehended that to keep so large and unique a project – one that required the presence on-site of hundreds of workmen for several years – completely secret, was quite impossible.

The secrecy dilemma posed other problems too, for it meant that SUBTERFUGE could never be properly tested. If it were to be fully, or even partially, manned for exercise or its communications systems operated during peacetime then its secrecy would be fatally compromised. The MGW Planning Team was aware of the bunkers currently under construction for NATO and the American administration in the United States, and drew unfavourable comparisons. Due to the nature of the topography of North America, the government there was able to build highly secure bunkers deep inside mountains and protected by more than two thousand feet of hard rock. In the United

Kingdom the geology was not so favourable and the British central government bunker, by now re-named STOCKWELL, was protected by no more than one hundred feet of relatively soft limestone. In the United States, too, there was funding available for such vast projects, whereas in cash-strapped Britain there was not. Speaking of the American model, the Planning Team commented that:

> 'The solution adopted consists partly of the construction of extremely deep headquarters under hills or mountains. Even on the basis of present knowledge and present designs these possess a degree of safety far beyond anything at STOCKWELL and it is conceivable that further research may make it possible to make them safe even against direct hits with large weapons. This, of course, is of the highest importance in that it resolves the dilemma of secrecy versus efficiency which haunts planning in this country: there would be no obstacle to such a physically secure headquarters being given its full communications in peacetime and thoroughly exercised.'

The potential cost of an American-style headquarters, even if the money was available and the nation's geology allowed it, raised a uniquely British political difficulty. Acutely aware that the British government was making little or no substantive provision for the protection of the general population, the MGW Sub-Committee noted that:

> 'To offer complete protection against the type of attack envisaged on the United Kingdom a shelter would have to be 2,000 feet underground in rock. No such site was known to exist in the United Kingdom and to prepare one would take a long time and would be extremely expensive (estimated at £10 million or more) and could not be kept secret. The fact that it could not be kept secret might give rise to embarrassing questions on other Civil Defence measures.'

By the end of 1960, with construction work at STOCKWELL well advanced, there were rumblings from the security services that the Soviet Union might already be aware of its existence, although this was largely discounted by the Cabinet Office under the confident assumption that the secrecy surrounding its planning and construction was as perfect as could possibly be attained. These concerns did, however, raise the issue that if the Russians were aware of STOCKWELL's existence, and if it was destroyed by enemy action before the decision to activate it had been taken, then there would be no nucleus from which government decisions could be disseminated. On the other hand, if the bunker were manned in the precautionary period and was then destroyed, central government, having all its eggs in one basket, would be wiped out at a stroke.

Faced with the twin scenarios of STOCKWELL either rendered useless by its secret being exposed, or by its destruction in a Soviet first strike, the MGW Sub-Committee looked again, in January 1961, at the practicality of providing an alternative seat of government at QUADRANGLE.

The manning and functioning of a second reserve headquarters in addition to STOCKWELL presented serious problems. In the precautionary period ministers and senior staff were likely to be fully stretched at Whitehall in preparing for war and in manning both STOCKWELL and the various Regional Headquarters. It was unlikely, therefore, that many staff could be spared to man QUADRANGLE on a purely standby basis. Also, it would have been difficult to keep QUADRANGLE fully informed of all developments during the precautionary stage and attack period. QUADRANGLE could not perform all the functions of STOCKWELL, partly because of its smaller size and partly because some parts of the organisation at STOCKWELL, the Shipping Control for example, could not be duplicated. During these periods control from QUADRANGLE would be sketchy at best and much responsibility would devolve upon the Regional Commissioners who, it was envisaged, would be of ministerial status. It was thought that it would nevertheless be worthwhile having some central control at a second alternative location in order to co-ordinate the activities of the Regional Commissioners and, later, to form a nucleus around which a full central government organisation would re-establish itself during the early post-attack phase, should the primary alternative headquarters have been destroyed. National control of food and fuel would have been particularly important during the immediate post-attack phase and it would have been these, along with essential services such as water supply, transport, communications and the resuscitation of key industries, with which staff at QUADRANGLE would be mainly concerned.

In light of the manning difficulties that had been highlighted it was suggested that the Regional Commissioner for the Midlands region, who would be housed in the regional seat of government co-located with QUADRANGLE at Drakelow should take the reins of central government should STOCKWELL cease to function. The emphasis in staffing would be towards the 'due-functioning' departments but there would be need also for at least a minimal input from the other departments, particularly the Foreign & Commonwealth Office and the armed services. In general, however, wide administrative experience was deemed more valuable than detailed but constrained departmental knowledge. Should STOCKWELL survive, then it was hoped that the small central government staff at QUADRANGLE could be of assistance to the Regional Commissioner in some undefined role.

By August 1961, by which time, as we have previously seen, the code-name of the headquarters had changed to BURLINGTON, the situation regarding its future remained unresolved. The continuing security concerns were crystallised in a report prepared by the MGW Planning Team which suggested that the need for a second alternative seat of government might arise if:

'There might be a known breach in the security of BURLINGTON; a breach so definite that it would become foolish to use it at all. Or, less disastrously, its security might be judged likely to become so suspect in the course of time that a second centre should be prepared in advance as an assurance.

'The decision to move to BURLINGTON (on the basis of present plans) is politically so difficult, and the disturbance to the smooth working of Whitehall so great (at a moment when this is supremely important) that it is possible that the decision might be taken too late. Hence there may be a case for a second headquarters designed on a scale free from these disadvantages: a headquarters that could be manned inconspicuously by a small number of senior officials without much upsetting Whitehall in advance of, and without prejudice to, any subsequent decision to man BURLINGTON.

'We attach much weight to both these considerations. As regards the first, our feeling is that however careful we are about disseminating knowledge of BURLINGTON and however cunning with cover stories, decoys, etc., the security of an establishment of its size and nature is, inevitably, a wasting asset. If it disappears we find ourselves with no Central Government Headquarters for use in nuclear war at all, and we would submit that this is an unacceptable risk. We do not, however, draw the inference that a second Headquarters of comparable size should be constructed. This is not only because it would be expensive and take a long time: it is even more because the same security problems would arise sooner or later. We doubt if two BURLINGTONS would be more secure than one. Thus a second Headquarters must, in our view, be on a much smaller scale. For the reasons given above we also believe that such a second establishment needs to be considered, and we recommend it even if the security of BURLINGTON were impregnable.'

It was argued that only if the second reserve headquarters was kept very small would it have any chance of being fully equipped with communications and be kept in a fit state for immediate activation without extreme risk to its security. Also, it was thought that a small headquarters could be successfully manned for exercises without attracting attention. A working figure of about 300 personnel was suggested; this number, it was thought, could be got in and out of the bunker inconspicuously and the staff might be successfully drilled not to divulge their experience. On the other hand, after once being filled and emptied again, BURLINGTON's security would undoubtedly disappear.

The Planning Team concluded that a complement of the size suggested above might be despatched to QUADRANGLE during the precautionary period and that its possible alternative role was to be either useless, because the emergency had evaporated or BURLINGTON had been successfully activated or, secondly, to take charge of the central direction of government if London and BURLINGTON were wiped out. Their report went on to conclude that:

'There could of course be no pretence that such a party could perform in the same way as the group, many times as large, envisaged for BURLINGTON, but the team assume:

- That some pre-established centre from which communication with foreign governments could be effected is essential.
- That at least some liaison between an Acting Prime Minister and the Armed Forces must be preserved in the survival period.
- That some possibility of co-ordination between Regional Headquarters through however tiny a Central Government is worth ensuring.
- That a predetermined centre round which a Central Government of a less minimal kind could grow by accretion would be of value in the survival and recovery period.'

Much thought was given to the communications facilities that would be required at QUADRANGLE. It was stressed that, in order not to arouse suspicion, these should be kept to a minimum and as far as possible should be consistent with those services that might be required by a Regional Government Headquarters. The GPO, who were responsible for communications planning, suggested that where more than one Private Wire ran from BURLINGTON to a distant terminal one should be routed through the telephone repeater station (probably the hardened structure recently built at Lyndon Green near Birmingham), serving QUADRANGLE so that it could be diverted. Because the role of QUADRANGLE, which would only become operational in a post-strike situation in which the primary seat of government was destroyed, would be relevant only to the survival and recovery period, communications facilities at BURLINGTON mainly planned for the precautionary and destructive periods would not be required there.

Quickly discounting the notions of creating an alternative emergency seat of government in the form of a mobile column of vehicles, or as a ship-board headquarters, the MGW Planning Team concluded that QUADRANGLE was 'as good a site as is now available'. Based upon this advice the chairman of the MGW Sub-Committee on 4 August 1961 recommended to its parent Home Defence Committee that preparation of a detail plan for QUADRANGLE should be put in hand. However, other than an inevitable change of code-name, this time from QUADRANGLE to LINSTOCK, no further material progress was made with the scheme.

The TURNSTILE years – 1963 to 1970

On 25 January 1963 those who needed to know were informed by the MGW Sub-Committee that 'the project for a reserve government headquarters in war will henceforward be known by the code-word TURNSTILE.'

Although there were no treasury funds available to proceed with the recently renamed second-eleven bunker at LINSTOCK, the MGW Sub-Committee continued to fret about the vulnerability of not only TURNSTILE but LINSTOCK too. Indeed, the whole concept of large (or relatively small, as in the case of LINSTOCK) fixed emergency headquarters at specific, fixed locations was cast into doubt. The rapidity with which the Cuban missile crisis had developed rather frightened the British establishment into believing that – ignoring for the moment all the other logistic, political and manpower problems that might be involved – come the probably inevitable war with the Soviet Union, missiles would rain down upon London long before the dilatory decision-makers could make the judgement to evacuate central government to one or other of its secret concrete redoubts.

In 1962 the first inkling of a multi-element, fragmented dispersal scheme of central government began to emerge. This concept continued to evolve, reappearing in different guises over the next five decades, and appears to survive in some vague way today. The first iteration of this plan, code-named TACK, involved the creation of a series of small central-government-headquarters-in-waiting, located

at a number of the Regional Seats of Government then nearing completion. Initially four sites were earmarked: Dover, where the RSG was constructed in part of the Second World War tunnel system; at Hope Cove, an RSG created in the underground control bunker of a recently decommissioned early Cold War era radar station on the South Devon coast; at Reading, in the early 1950s Regional War Room, and at Shipton in North Yorkshire where another underground radar control room was being refurbished as a regional seat of government. In the event of London becoming untenable and both TURNSTILE and LINSTOCK being destroyed, the surviving TACK sites, which were regarded as a series of third-line reserves of central government, could have nominally, in a pre-determined order, 'gathered the reigns of central direction'.

The TACK complement at each RSG amounted to only thirty-two officials headed by a Deputy Reserve Prime Minister, one Minister and two Private Secretaries, but despite its small size it was soon discovered that there was insufficient room for them at any of the chosen RSGs. At Dover it was thought that they might be able to squeeze a further twenty TACK personnel in alongside the regional government contingent but at Hope Cove there was no space available (indeed, the bunker had insufficient capacity even for its planned regional government contingent), and both Shipton and Reading, which were currently still under preparation, reported that they too were unlikely to have spare capacity. The problem of lack of capacity at the proposed sites was quickly compounded by a recent security analysis which suggested that the Russians were aware of the locations of the Regional Seats of Government, the construction of which was not concealed behind the same fog of secrecy as TURNSTILE, and that they were probably high on the target list. It was then assumed that the Soviet intelligence service, aware of the locations and functions of the Regional Seats of Government, would deduce the TACK concept and that assumption alone would be sufficient for them to be considered high priority targets. Given the mounting problems, together with the general unwillingness of an increasingly cash-strapped Treasury to fund any increase in the civil defence budget, it was announced in November 1963 that no further expenditure on TACK sites would be authorised.

In the wave of post-Cuba paranoia that had given rise to TACK, the MGW Sub-Committee was warned that the Russians, although not directly aware of the location of TURNSTILE, were probably aware of the fact that the Hawthorn area of Corsham housed an unusual concentration of communications facilities some of which, perhaps unknown to them, were associated with TURNSTILE and would in certain circumstances be vital in the process of authorising nuclear retaliation. Thus an attack on these facilities might, as a more-or-less collateral consequence, destroy TURNSTILE or, if not, at least reduce its capacity to authorise timely retribution. The committee's response was to minute that 'since security is vital for TURNSTILE (or any plan that succeeds it – other than a genuinely invulnerable redoubt) it becomes imperative to take a decision about its future.' Possible alternative courses of action to follow included 'the concept of adopting a completely different type of organisation that would be based from the start on dispersal, and even mobility.' Having invested so heavily in the Corsham project, however, the committee was loath to discard it completely and recommended in May 1963 that 'under any alternative plan something would still remain at TURNSTILE because it is too valuable an installation to abandon entirely. One point for examination will be the extent to which it might still be possible to preserve TURNSTILE, for as long as we can, as a cover story for the new plan. This in itself will be helped if we can keep it in the plan but as something other than the potential central seat of government.'

WELLRIGHT & MALLARD

When detailed plans for the organisation of the Central Government War Headquarters were first prepared, the government somewhat naively included within it accommodation for representatives from two NATO agencies, the NATO Oil Executive Board (NOEB) and the Defence Shipping Executive Board (DSEB), agencies which were to become increasingly important as post-attack survival planning developed to maturity. By 1962 a number of problems had arisen which were to some extent frustrate the government's plans. Locating the Eastern Hemisphere divisional headquarters of the two agencies had involved difficult negotiations, particularly with the French, who resented the concentration of such potential post-war power and influence in the United Kingdom. A contemporary discussion paper commented that: 'The French think our control over the agencies will be too strong and, for that reason, have been sticky over their financing. Undoubtedly, if they had a chance, they would seek to embarrass us, possibly by seeking the removal of the agencies themselves.' Britain's argument, however, was that of all the European countries she was the only one with an existing, protected emergency central government infrastructure in which safely to house the oil and shipping boards. In a letter to Sir Norman Brook, the Cabinet Secretary, it was explained that:

'Other members of NATO tacitly recognise that the UK is the main directing centre in the eastern hemisphere of international oil movements in peacetime, and that we have the majority of the experts; so that there would be least disturbance and least danger of a hiatus after nuclear attack if experts already on the spot in the UK exercising a similar function in wartime, subject to broad political control by NOEB. We hope, therefore, to get agreement to a technical staff which is preponderantly British and which makes only modest concessions to the national sentiment of the other members. The French in particular, however, are suspicious of the UK in this matter, and if NOEB were shifted to another country, probably France, I fear that the staff would be recruited on the basis of nationality, with detriment to both UK interests and to good management. Once this had happened, its effects would be felt right through the survival and recovery periods.

'I think it is also worth taking into account that surviving international channels of communications are likely to be congested, so that if NOEB were in this country we should have an advantage over other countries. Indeed, there may be more subtle ways in which UK influence could be exerted over NOEB in this country which would not be possible if it were situated elsewhere.'

Somewhat strangely, when this situation was reviewed in January 1962 the Home Defence Committee could not be sure why the NOEB and DSEB had ever been offered accommodation at BURLINGTON, commenting in the discussion paper that 'it is likely that the reason why the agencies were put in BURLINGTON was because the site was large enough to take them and it would be convenient to have them with the rest of our top-level staff.' The document went on to say that: 'we have got a lot of prestige from the fact that our accommodation is ready for activation and NATO has thereby been stirred on to efforts in other directions.'

The problem was that soon after the plans were made the Home Defence Committee realised that the foreign members of the boards would be, in part at least, of high-ranking diplomatic status who would expect unlimited and uncensored communications facilities with their own embassies elsewhere in the world and with their own national governments. The British government, however, were convinced that whilst Britain's internal security was water-tight, that of most foreign countries leaked like sieves and that uncensored diplomatic traffic from within BURLINGTON would inevitably give away the secrets of its location and purpose and destroy its capacity to function. Obviously, it was politically impossible to tell the foreign representatives that they were not thought trustworthy, although the British government toyed with the idea of censoring their communications in a clandestine manner.

Two other related problems compounded the government's difficulties with the NATO agencies. The first was that NATO expected to be able to run peacetime exercises including the NOEB and DSEB; the second was that NATO intended to activate both agencies on the declaration of a Simple Alert, some time before the commencement of hostilities, whereas the British government was unlikely to authorise the activation of BURLINGTON until the very last moment. Although NATO and certain foreign governments knew that Britain had an emergency headquarters they did not know its size, capability or location, and the British government was not prepared to disclose such information, at least until after hostilities had ceased. Therefore, exercises or early manning were out of the question.

The latter difficulties, however, gave the Home Defence Committee the excuse they needed to take measures to counter the threat of accidental disclosure by the foreign diplomatic representatives. The only viable solution was to relocate the agencies elsewhere, either with or without informing NATO of the reasons for the change. In March 1963, (by which time the Corsham headquarters had undergone yet another change of code-name to TURNSTILE), partial agreement was reached upon the approach that should be taken. A note from the Home Office, which was involved in the evolution of this plan, suggested:

'Attention might be drawn to our inability, so long as the agencies are at TURNSTILE, to bring our allies into closer consultation on the preparation of the headquarters, to allow visits by representatives of member nations or the International Staff, to hold exercises on site, or even provide detailed information about the facilities available.'

The document continued by saying:

'This could lead to an explanation that the United Kingdom recognises fully that these agencies are of vital concern to the Alliance as a whole and is anxious that these difficulties should be removed so as to permit the maximum co-operation in planning and preparation by all member nations.'

There would inevitably be difficulties in implementing this policy,

as a representative of the Ministry of Power pointed out, drawing attention to:

'... the attitude in recent months of the French Government, who have made it plain that they suspect the United Kingdom of trying to gain too great an influence over the agencies in this country in war. The French have already attempted for this reason to block the appointment of a United Kingdom nominee to a key post in the eastern branch of the NATO wartime oil organisation and the Ministry fear that if NATO is now told that we propose to alter the location of the headquarters, the French will seize the opportunity to press for establishing the executive boards in France. The announcement of a fresh start would in any event lose the credit which at present accrues to the United Kingdom from being the only host country with agency accommodation fully prepared.'

By this time a decision had been taken that the former mustard gas storage tunnels at Rhydymwyn, the third of the Second World War underground factory sites described earlier in this book, would be developed as the alternative headquarters for NOEB and DSEB. For this proposed role, the Rhydymwyn tunnels were given the code-name WELLBRIGHT. Various arguments were put forwards as to whether work on the site should be completed and Britain's allies then led to believe that Rhydymwyn was, in fact, TURNSTILE, or whether it would be admitted that it was a separate, remote location solely for the use of the NATO agencies. To take the former course, it was decided, was too risky and could lead to considerable embarrassment. With regard to the second course of action, three alternatives were proposed:

- Work should be completed on site before NATO was informed. This, it was thought, might be interpreted, and resented, as presenting member countries with a fait accompli.
- To inform NATO of the change of location as soon as Parliamentary authority for the work was obtained.
- To defer an announcement to NATO until sufficient work had been done on the site to render it presentable. This, it was thought, was subject to the serious objection that heavy expenditure would be necessary to put the site into a presentable condition and this expenditure might be wasted if member countries were to find the proposed change to the accommodation unacceptable.

As an aside, it was noted in a letter to Lieutenant Colonel Paget at the Cabinet Office that:

'If the role of the agencies at WELLBRIGHT is vital in the survival phase, as I understand to be the opinion of the departments primarily concerned, we think that the project should be classified 'Top Secret' and that when the time comes to release the information to NATO it should be released as 'Cosmic Top Secret' on as limited a basis as possible. A possible argument for giving it the higher classification is that it would be embarrassing to the UK should any leakage occur before we are ready to release the information to NATO.'

By this time the Home Defence Committee had convinced themselves that the course of action they were embarking upon was a legitimate one, a member commenting that:

'NATO should be told that 'the NOEB would be housed in the complex of Government-protected accommodation, and that it would not be necessary to specify whether their accommodation was to be at TURNSTILE or somewhere else. Sir Robert Harvey had previously mentioned that the wartime communications from the Valley tunnels to foreign countries would have to be directed through TURNSTILE, and I said that this reinforced my view that the two places could be bracketed together as one complex of linked Government accommodation.'

This, though, was not the end of the government's difficulties. Almost immediately it was discovered that the Ministry of Works, who were in the process of taking over responsibility for the Rhydymwyn tunnels from the War Office, had promised them to the Bank of England as an emergency storage site for the nation's gold reserves. At much the same time, the Home Office had been in negotiation with the War Office and, rather belatedly with the Ministry of Works, with a view to adapting the tunnels as a regional seat of government for Wales. On top of this, Imperial Chemical Industries Ltd, which had operated the tunnels and adjacent factory during the Second World War, expressed an interest in acquiring the tunnels for the storage of explosives. Thus, a compound and embarrassing conflict of interests emerged and protracted negotiations began.

The requirements of the Home Office were dismissed with little ceremony and it seemed that an agreement could be made between the Cabinet Office, representing the NATO agencies, and the Bank of England, over shared occupancy. Later, however, it was discovered that the Home Defence Committee wished to co-locate the national Shipping Authority as well as the NATO Shipping Agency and the NOEB at WELLBRIGHT. A Home Defence Committee briefing paper circulated in January 1963 explained the situation:

Above: The outer-most section of No.2 entrance tunnel at Rhydymwyn. Had the WELLBRIGHT scheme gone ahead this tunnel, and all the others, would have been partitioned lengthwise to facilitate the provision of a large number of offices with narrow access corridors between.

Below: A typical lateral storage tunnel at Rhydymwyn. The grilles in the centre of the tunnel cover deep drainage ducts. In the area earmarked for the storage of the Bank of England gold reserves plans were prepared to construct reinforced concrete platforms across the drainage voids to support the weight of the gold bullion.

Above: The abandoned *ROTOR* radar control room at St. Twynnells in the Pembroke Peninsula. This two-storey structure (one of which is below ground) was proposed as an alternative refuge for the nation's gold reserves.

'The total area at the Valley Tunnels site is about 80,000 square feet and apart from the Shipping Authority and the two NATO Agencies there have been two other bids for accommodation there. The first is from the Home Office who had it in mind to occupy 20,000 square feet for a Sub-Regional Headquarters and who will now have to look elsewhere, and the second is from the Bank of England who wanted 30,000 square feet for their project known as MALLARD. The Bank have confirmed that though their first preference is for the entire 30,000 square feet at Valley Tunnels they would not object to a division of their requirements between Valley Tunnels and some other place provided such other place was reasonably accessible and generally suitable. In fact, another place of 20,000 square feet (the recently decommissioned semi-underground *ROTOR* radar control centre at St. Twynnells) is available and is being held against possible requirement by the Bank which has not, however, yet inspected it. The Home Office have said that St. Twynnells is not suitable for their Sub-Regional Headquarters but the Bank's needs are less exacting.'

Discussions continued inconclusively for two or three years by which time the problem of the NATO agencies had been overtaken by the complete revision of Home Defence planning and the birth of the PYTHON scheme of smaller, dispersed, flexible and widely distributed emergency government nodes, described in more detail below. A review of available underground sites conducted by the Ministry of Public Building and Works in August 1968 concluded that, as far as the Home Office and the NATO agencies were concerned 'interest in the Valley Tunnels as a location for either of these organisations is now virtually dead.' However, the Bank of England, which was still searching for a suitable wartime location for its gold reserves, remained marginally interested. In a letter to the Cabinet Office dated 6 August 1968 a Ministry of Public Building and Works (MPBW) officer explained first that the scheme earlier known by the code-name MALLARD was now referred to as FOLIUM, and then went on to outline the current situation:

'We know that FOLIUM is a plan to store 3,700 tons of gold in a space of 30,000 square feet stacked to four feet high. Underground storage is envisaged at a depth of around 100 feet because of the danger of vaporisation from a thermo-nuclear explosion in the vicinity. Other stipulations of the Bank of England are that the accommodation should provide for the unloading and turn-around of 250 ten-ton lorries every two days for a week, ideally under cover, at a location within the radii from London to Lincoln or Malvern. No special environmental conditions are necessary, only basic provision for accommodating guards.'

The general consensus appeared to have been that the tunnels at Rhydymwyn were unsuitable because it was not considered wise to transport such a valuable commodity over such a long distance from London at the Precautionary Stage. Instead it was suggested that the MGW Sub-Committee should look again at the possibility of using for the storage of the gold reserves one of the other government owned quarries in the Corsham area, including the recently decommissioned Central Ammunition Depots at Eastlays, Monkton Farleigh and Tunnel Quarry, or the art treasures repository at Westwood Quarry, a disused stone quarry near Bradford-on-Avon in Wiltshire, all of which had been discounted in 1963. John Brown, for the MPBW, made the point that 'a journey by rail from Mount Pleasant via Paddington and straight into Tunnel Quarry, (which had its own dedicated branch line entering the underground workings at the east end of Box Tunnel on the London to Bristol main line), looks the most attractive from the point of view of both security and swiftness of journey.' In reply, Wing Commander Hermitage, on behalf of the Cabinet Office, commented:

> 'I take John Brown's point about the difficulty of moving such a valuable commodity over a long distance. However, I do not entirely favour his idea of the Box stone mines or Tunnel Quarry in case they should prove to be nuclear targets. But I agree the train would be a good method of transport and storage if we could find a suitable tunnel. Perhaps we should start from scratch again in planning this operation and suggest alternative methods of transport and sites when we raise the question in MGW.'

Upon this somewhat inconclusive note discussion of an alternative wartime location for the nation's gold reserves appears to have petered out, although there were passing references in the 1980s to the possibility of utilising one of the areas of TURNSTILE rendered redundant by the proposed 'reduced-area' scheme. Similarly, brief consideration was given to storing the national art treasures in the same location. During the Second World War, after the failure of a seemingly successful but ultimately abortive scheme to house the art treasures in a number of country houses in the provinces, all the pictures from the National Gallery eventually found their way to Manod Quarry, an underground slate mine high in the Snowdon mountains. Everything else, including all the artefacts from all of London's other museums and galleries were gathered together in Westwood Quarry near Bradford-on-Avon. During the early Cold War years (up, indeed, until the early 1980s) the government retained a lien on these two quarries and in 1964 a scheme, code-named METHODICAL, was put in place to once again utilise these quarries in event of a nuclear war. Planned on a smaller scale than the previous evacuation, METHODICAL envisaged the transport of selected items

from the National Gallery, the National Portrait Gallery, the Tate Gallery and the Royal Collection to Manod Quarry, with a similar selection from the British Museum, the Public Records Office, the Guildhall Library, the Victoria & Albert Museum and the Wallace Collection going to Westwood Quarry. Transport would be arranged by the Ministry of Public Building and Works and would involve eleven pantechnicons; rather less than the fleets of lorries and special trains involved in the earlier operation.

PYTHON *in ascendancy*

Unable to come to a firm decision regarding the future of the Corsham site, which was coming to be seen increasingly as an alarmingly expensive yet possibly indispensable white elephant, the Cabinet Office appears to have continued a parallel, two-track approach. Construction and fitting-out continued at TURNSTILE in a desultory way while at the same time detailed plans were being prepared for a system of dispersed central government cells that was conceptually the polar opposite of the original SUBTERFUGE scheme. The new approach, code-named PYTHON, was initiated in June 1964 but not authorised by the Prime Minister until May 1968. It envisaged 'a scheme of dispersal involving a number of groups, each with the power to take over the functions of central government in war, self-sufficient and in pre-arranged order of priority, which would be determined by the seniority of the Minister in charge of each group.' Each PYTHON group would consist of up to 150 members. Very little has been disclosed regarding the composition, function, location or even number of these groups, although it has been estimated that in the early planning phase between five and thirteen groups were envisaged. By 1982 the number of PYTHON groups was reduced to four, supported by three United Kingdom Supply Agency (UKSA) groups and three National Air Transport Agency (NATA) groups.

The scenario upon which the PYTHON scheme was predicated assumed that in the immediate aftermath of nuclear war a third of the nation's population would die, the bulk of Britain's industrial capacity would be destroyed, communications – both inland and overseas – would be severely disrupted for several days at least, and perhaps for an extended period, and central government from London would cease to exist. Current planning acknowledged that the limited capability of the surviving elements of government would be to endeavour to ensure little more than the bare survival of the remaining population. There was, however, a political motive too (in the broadest sense of the phrase) for, within Whitehall, overt evidence of the continuity of government was of equal importance to national survival. Reflecting this, a Cabinet Office draft memorandum from the time noted that 'it is an essential part of HMG's planning for war that a legally constituted Government of the United Kingdom should remain in being continuously in order to direct Britain's struggle for survival and to conduct her relations with the rest of the world through the British Overseas Authorities.'

PYTHON sought to remedy the weaknesses inherent in previous schemes of central government evacuation to a single, comprehensive, embunkered core alternative location, whilst at the same time recognising both the financial constraints that must be imposed upon any such scheme and the palpable reduction in belligerency between the western and eastern blocks that developed during the later years of the 1960s. The fact that having all one's eggs in one basket at Corsham would be catastrophic if the bunker was destroyed once it became manned and operational was obvious, as was the fact that the catastrophe would be equally as absolute if the bunker-occupants-designate were wiped out before they made it to Corsham. The scale of catastrophe would be only little diminished if the Corsham headquarters, with its concentrated hub of vital communications facilities, was turned to ash and vapour before it could be put to use. The latter was a difficulty that with ingenuity and imagination might be overcome; the former setbacks would inevitably prove terminal. PYTHON however, as we shall see, was and still remains subject to its own grave shortcomings.

A pivotal weakness of every stage of the United Kingdom's Cold War emergency planning was the assumption that protected cores of government, either central or regional could without question, by the exercise of sanctions, maintain authority, command the will of the people at home, retain the loyalty of its overseas dominions and dependencies and the support of friendly foreign powers. In reality, the probability was that a claustrophobic, compact concentration of civil servants contained within the confines of a subterranean bunker at Corsham could do little more than squabble amongst themselves, for they had no viable means to either project their power or encourage civil compliance.

PYTHON sought to remedy all these difficulties by means of dispersion and devolution. Dispersion was a key element at all levels on the home front and also with the surviving government's relations with overseas authorities. At a time of crisis central government would be divided into a number of small PYTHON groups that would

be dispersed throughout the country. Each would be led by a Minister of cabinet rank and each would be, essentially, a micro-government-in-waiting. It was hoped that, by being widely dispersed, at least two, and hopefully more, of the groups would survive and that within fourteen to thirty days of a nuclear strike the surviving elements would coalesce to form the core of a viable administrative structure. Immediately after the strike, the senior surviving group would identify itself to its peers, to the surviving Regional Commissioners and to the world at large as the legally constituted central government of the United Kingdom. Where the coalescence, or 'accretion', would occur would depend upon what facilities had survived the initial attack but, as we will see below, it was hoped that Corsham would escape the holocaust and, indeed, preparations would have been put in hand during the escalatory phase of the war to make it ready for the arrival of its post-attack contingent. Whatever other contingency plans had been made, through the agency of the military CONRAD radio communications system or whatever, the only dependable, hardened international communications facility remained at Corsham, and without it the vestigial central government organisation would have been severely disadvantaged.

Although dispersal overcame one major stumbling block, its inevitably diminished communications capability created others which could have been critical during the crucial two-week period of predicted utter dislocation immediately following a nuclear attack. For the senior surviving PYTHON group, for example, attempting to make contact from an unknown location with Regional Government Headquarters that may or may not have survived, and with overseas posts via fragile communications links that would more likely than not have been destroyed, the mere process of identifying itself as the legitimate national government and ultimate source of authority would have been a prodigious task. Thereafter, the ability to exercise any real power from a position of such obvious weakness would have been debatable.

The initial dispersal of the central government elements was also reflected in similar dispersal plans for both the regional government emergency scheme and for the organisation of British diplomatic posts overseas. At home, the long-established hierarchical scheme of Regional Government Headquarters and Sub-Regional Controls, with various local government controls below them, all provided with hardened bunkers, was thoroughly overhauled. A policy document issued in November 1973 provides a résumé of current thinking:

'All planning for the post-attack situation is for the Survival

Period, i.e. the period between the end of the Life Saving Period and the time it proves possible to resume central government. This period might be a minimum of ninety days; it could be a matter of years. The assumptions are that the nuclear attack will be of varying degrees of severity in its effects on the structure of civilised life over the country as a whole; that devastation will not be total and that it will be possible to restore some sort of normal life in at least some areas. During the Survival Period the day-to-day administration will be in the hands of twelve autonomous Regional Governments and their sub-controls, each Regional Government under a senior cabinet minister and staffed with representatives of the principal government departments. The sites for Regional Seats of Government will not be established until after the attack.'

Only a relatively small nucleus would man each of the hardened Sub-Regional Control bunkers; the much larger staff that would operate the survival period regional seat of government would have been found temporary accommodation during the precautionary phase in widely dispersed hotels or government owned buildings in the broad vicinity of the S-RCs. It was hoped that these could be made to some extent fallout-proof, but exactly how this was to be done was never specified. Those of the hotel dwellers who survived would, after the attack, find suitable office accommodation (again unspecified) in which to set up a viable Regional Government Headquarters which may have been called upon to function more-or-less autonomously for several months or even years. The pertinent points of this plan were that:

- A large number of civil servants would be required adequately to administer the regional seat of government, and that their best chance of survival while under attack and while waiting to take up their allotted post-strike tasks was to be widely dispersed.

- It was accepted that a small nucleus of civil servants, no matter how illustrious their rank, would be utterly impotent and unable to command authority while holed-up in a concrete bunker and would, indeed, be more likely to engender resentment rather than co-operation in such a situation. Under such circumstances, government and policing could only be accomplished by consent and that could be achieved only by having an open and accessible organisation located in an approachable surface headquarters.

PYTHON also recognised the pivotal importance of Britain's overseas diplomatic organisation during the initial phase of the recovery period. Rather belatedly it was realised that the supply of food and

fuel oil were by far the most important responsibilities of central government in the post-apocalyptic world, and equally belatedly government realised that a small (or even a large) coterie of civil servants ensconced within a bunker one hundred feet below a Wiltshire village was almost powerless in this respect. While the regional and local authority organisations could put feet on the ground to distribute resources if and when they were made available, it was largely left to Britain's overseas administrations to source the necessities of survival.

Abroad, a system of devolution and dispersal was, therefore, also implemented. Britain's overseas diplomatic representation was divided into seven regional groups, and within each group one was classified as the Leading Post. Leading Posts were selected largely for their access to Commonwealth, United States and Allied authorities and military commanders, their communications capacity within their regions, their size, staffing levels and prospect of survival. Two 'National Agencies' of central government would be set up to control respectively air transport, through the National Air Transport Agency (NATA) and sea transport and overseas supply through the United Kingdom Supplies Agency (UKSA). Procurement of supplies from overseas would be undertaken by the British overseas authorities, co-ordinated by the Leading Posts of the various overseas groups. *Instructions to Leading Posts* noted that:

'A vital task in the survival and reconstruction phase would be the resupply of the United Kingdom with food and raw materials from Commonwealth and Foreign countries. The importance of the part to be played by British overseas authorities needs no emphasis; if adequate supplies were not to reach this devastated country after a nuclear attack the nation would cease to exist.'

The instructions went on to detail the nation's food requirements from overseas sources and outlined the roles of Ministry of Agriculture, Fisheries and Food overseas procurement agents who would collaborate with the British overseas authorities, but admitted that no such officers actually existed other than tea procurement agents in Ceylon and India. Oil supply, second only in importance to food, would be left in the hands of the oil industry, working in collaboration with UKSA but with little input from the Ministry of Power. Although a memorandum prepared by the Cabinet Office ahead of the release of the *Instructions To Leading Posts* commented that 'in each PYTHON group there would be staff from the Diplomatic Service to conduct overseas affairs and the highest importance is attached to the continued functioning of our posts overseas because on them would depend the success of the re-supply operation,' it was made clear in the Instructions that the Leading Posts may well have been required to act solely upon their own initiatives for a considerable time. How these overseas supplies would be paid for remained a largely unanswered question. The problem was addressed thus in the *Instructions to Leading Posts*:

'It is not yet possible to give overseas posts any clear guidance on how the operations described in the memorandum would be paid for, largely because it is impossible to say what any country's money would be worth after a global nuclear conflagration. It might be some time before anything like a recognised system of international exchange and payments could be re-established. In the last resort British overseas authorities would be expected to pledge Britain's credit anywhere it was acceptable in order to fulfil the tasks allotted to them.'

In the event of the almost total disruption of communications in a Britain devastated by nuclear attack, the overseas posts would play a major role in the gathering of information about the world-wide repercussions of the war. They would also act as a source of propaganda regarding the state of the home nation. The *Instructions to Leading Posts* reminds them that:

'One of the first requirements of the survivor United Kingdom Government would be information on the state of the rest of the world. Major policy decisions would depend on a knowledge of any military operations continuing overseas, and of the state of war damage and public morale in other countries. The UK Government would also need to know urgently how other countries have aligned themselves in the conflict and what action, civil or military, they were prepared to take in support of their alignment.'

The document then goes on to say that:

'It will also be important to HMG in the United Kingdom, in its conduct of overseas affairs, that other countries should have as much authoritative information as possible about the situation in the United Kingdom, particularly in relation to the will to prosecute the struggle, the state of public morale, the existence of a constitutional government in the United Kingdom, and the efforts towards survival and reconstruction.'

The Cabinet Office attitude towards the Leading Posts was somewhat dichotomous; on the one hand they stressed how pivotal to Britain's survival their role would be during the aftermath of a nuclear war, yet on the other hand they went through enormously convoluted hoops

to ensure that the details of the PYTHON concept should be kept secret from them. In a minute to the Foreign and Commonwealth Office, the Cabinet Office wrote:

'As you are aware, knowledge of this delicate subject has been restricted by the Cabinet Office to a very limited number of officials on the need-to-know basis and you will no doubt wish this security point to be borne in mind when discussions take place in your Division.'

Elsewhere, during the drafting of the Instructions, it is stated that:

'Details of these dispersal plans are among the most vital of Britain's state secrets, their success being dependant on their total secrecy. British Overseas Authorities need only know that in the event of Whitehall being destroyed it is planned that the government of the United Kingdom shall continue to function constitutionally *from a dispersal site*.'

The italicised phrase '*from a dispersal site*' was seized upon by the security services and expunged from the final text on the grounds that it might provide a clue to the PYTHON secret. A similar point was raised at a meeting of the Home Defence Committee Machinery of Government in War Sub-Committee which considered early drafts of the Instructions. A contemporary memorandum commented that:

'The point was also made that certain phrases, notably 'survivor government' used in the instructions, might reveal the PYTHON concept of Central Government to the overseas posts. A comparison should be made between these instructions and the previous set of instructions in the light of the security requirement not to reveal the PYTHON concept to overseas posts.'

The reason for the almost paranoid secrecy regarding PYTHON, particularly in the context of the British Overseas Authorities, is difficult to fathom, for, at the same time, the Cabinet Office was giving consideration to the possibility that under certain circumstances authorisation for the release of nuclear weapons might be delegated to the Overseas Authorities. The probable answer is that whilst the PYTHON concept was designed to offer the greatest flexibility and probability of survival of at least some elements of central government, it suffered a fatal weakness in that for the short period immediately following an attack there would be no government and the country would be left effectively rudderless. Until one PYTHON group had identified itself, which would require a reliable means of communication (which the government had already admitted may well not have existed under the revised scheme) there would be no central administration to which dependant organisations – the regions, home and overseas military units and the British Overseas Authorities – could turn for guidance or instruction. There was no guarantee, either, that sufficient PYTHON groups would survive to form a viable government. There does, however, appear to have been a second objective underlying the PYTHON concept, and that was to provide protection for an admittedly weakened and vulnerable government from a secondary attack, either from an external enemy or from internal dissidence. This was made clear in a top secret memorandum issued in October 1980 which stated that, once the PYTHON plan had been implemented:

'Manpower and other resources allocated should be capable of maintaining readiness to come into operation (i.e. following a nuclear attack) for at least thirty days, *without exposing themselves to risk of discovery and attack.*'

The italicised final phrase is perhaps key to understanding the whole PYTHON concept.

TURNSTILE becomes CHANTICLEER

In the summer of 1975 (by which time TURNSTILE had become CHANTICLEER, the change in code-name having been authorised in 1970), the security agency MI5 began to fret that the CHANTICLEER secret was becoming too widely known. They were concerned that people who had no business to be concerned in such matters were concluding that because security at Corsham was becoming so apparently lax, then this was an indication that the site was of a lesser importance than hitherto and perhaps there was another secret location or locations that may have usurped its function. In a note to the Cabinet Office, MI5 commented that:

'Clearly a lot of individuals who do not have a need-to-know, know or have a very good idea of the original purpose of CHANTICLEER but whether this warrants the abandonment of the CHANTICLEER story is another matter. On the security side the major consideration is whether the abandonment of the CHANTICLEER cover-story would result in a greater effort to pinpoint the new 'selected areas' by those interested in obtaining such information.'

John Hutchinson, from the Cabinet Office, replied with considerable self-assurance 'effort maybe; result no!'

The following year another security scare was created by unauthorised aerial photography of the MoD estate at Corsham in connection with new surface building work being undertaken by

the Admiralty. This almost resulted in the abandonment of the new works (the construction of a new office block and computer centre on the Copenacre site), but it was argued that 're-provision elsewhere would weaken the general policy of retaining a large MoD presence in the Copenacre area as a cover for CHANTICLEER.'

The supposed advantage of the PYTHON concept was that it offered flexibility in the location of the groups, which were no longer tied to specific Regional Government Headquarters which, as we have seen, it was assumed were on the Soviet target list. However, it would appear that up until at least 1970 the support groups were designated fixed initial locations: UKSA groups, for example, were allocated to Bridge of Dun Barracks, Bovington Camp in Dorset, and to one of three Caledonian Macbrayne ferries, either Clansman, Hebrides or Columbia, which would have been fitted out as a floating operations centre. The three initial locations for the NATA groups were RAF Chivenor in Devon, RAF Llanbedr in Merionethshire, and Fort George Barracks at Inverness. Initial locations for the PYTHON groups have never been released although it has been implied that there were numerous alternative locations, possibly at remote, minor military establishments or government offices, to be occupied depending upon the prevailing conditions in the country. In the aftermath of attack, according to instructions issued in July 1967, 'the survivor government (i.e. the senior surviving PYTHON group) was to identify and authenticate itself' both to other central government components and to Leading Posts overseas. A few months earlier, in January 1967, during a discussion regarding the location of the NATO civil agencies, (DSEB and NOEB), it was noted that no firm decision could be made until it was decided whether or not a PYTHON group would be initially located at TURNSTILE. At that time the total manning level of DSEB was estimated at 380 and it was debated what proportion of these would be initially accommodated at TURNSTILE, the minute of the meeting recording that:

'It has always been the view of the Ministry of Transport that only a nucleus of this Agency should be initially located at TURNSTILE, the rest of the staff being distributed amongst the United Kingdom Regional Port and Shipping Headquarters until such time, post-attack, as it could appropriately be fully manned to undertake its full responsibilities. It was considered that a nucleus of 150 staff should be adequate to discharge the tasks of the Agency in the initial stages.'

At the meeting it was suggested that the strength of NOEB should be of the order of 100, who would all be together from the start.

The perceived advantage of not being tied to a particular location posed serious communications problems and gives rise to questions as to exactly how flexible the system would have been in practice. It has been suggested that, on the one hand, fixed telecommunications were installed at certain locations ready to receive PYTHON units, which would largely negate the concept of mobility, and on the other hand that the greater part of each group's communications would be provided by a mobile column of military vehicles operating the CONRAD radio communications system, which appears to introduce the twin disadvantages of vulnerability and unreliability. The CONRAD system was under the control of No.2 Signals Brigade, the headquarters of which was located at Corsham. The probability that fixed locations were earmarked for the PYTHON groups is indicated by a Cabinet Office document circulated in April 1980 concerning the cost of renting communications equipment from British Telecom at CHANTICLEER and elsewhere. The annual charge for equipment at TURNSTILE amounted to £96,000, while that for the PYTHON sites totalled £215,000, which indicates installations each of a considerable size.

As a consequence of the cutbacks in civil defence expenditure after 1968, maintenance at Corsham was reduced to a minimum. During this period the PYTHON scheme continued to evolve, but the Spring Quarry bunker maintained a key role in the plan despite the apparent reservations felt by the Home Defence Machinery of Government in War Sub-Committee. A key part of the concept was that in the post-strike period the surviving groups would reassemble or accrete at a single location which would then become the recognised seat of government. Although, in theory, this could be almost anywhere that suitable communications facilities with the regions and the rest of the world existed, the reality was that the only viable location was Corsham, with its immense inland and international communications infrastructure and administrative support facilities. Should the Corsham complex have been destroyed in the nuclear attack, then in all probability the surviving PYTHON groups would have been in a very weak position.

The persistently pivotal position of the underground complex at Corsham is made clear in the assumptions prefacing the record of an informal meeting of the MGW Sub-Committee in November 1978. In this document the committee assume that during the thirty-day precautionary period leading up to a nuclear attack, an advance party under command of a Camp Commandant, consisting of ninety-five civilian and military officers together with 160 other ranks, would

arrive at CHANTICLEER in order to prepare the communications equipment and ensure that all the plant and services were in operational order and ready to receive the executive staff. None of these initial personnel would perform any central government role and were essentially merely technicians. It was further assumed that within the thirty days following the attack at least two PYTHON groups would have reassembled at CHANTICLEER, together with two of the three UKSA groups, or one UKSA group and an ad-hoc group performing the same function. These would be assisted by a further ad-hoc group of 186 military and civilian personnel. The National Air Transport Agency (NATA) units would not head for CHANTICLEER in the post-attack phase but would continue to operate from their functional accommodation, which would probably be located at non-front-line RAF stations, probably in Wales or the West Country.

When the communications centre in Area 21 was initially set up in the early 1960s there were dedicated areas for all three fighting services, the Foreign & Colonial Office and the Home Defence departments, but in the CHANTICLEER plan of 1978 the communications contingent of the advance party does not include any Admiralty staff. Of the 138 members of each PYTHON group expected to accrete at CHANTICLEER, twenty-seven would oversee home affairs, fifty would be concerned with defence and overseas affairs, and sixty-one solely concerned with communications and general administration. Of each UKSA group, ninety were assigned to supplies procurement and the remaining forty-nine to communications and administration. Amongst the ad-hoc staff, fifty would be specialists in defence and overseas affairs, and forty-six experts in matters of home affairs.

The adoption of the PYTHON policy meant that the physical accommodation required at Corsham was reduced from that for a staff of approximately 4,000 to somewhere between 750 and 1,000, and thus it was possible to almost completely abandon much of the western half of the quarry. Between 1968 and 1970 the air-conditioning plant in Area 19 was shut down, the bakery, kitchen and dining facilities in areas 6 and 7 closed down and partially dismantled, and the laundry facilities in Area 20 abandoned, although some of the equipment was transferred to Area 12 in the east end of the quarry for use in the reconfigured headquarters. Areas 3, 4 and 5, allocated as dormitories but never fitted out, were also abandoned, along with the office facilities in areas 17 and 18. Area 2, earlier allocated to the Board of Trade and other 'due functioning' departments, was partitioned off and handed over to the RAF to become the 'Quarry Operations Centre' or QOC, details of which can be found elsewhere in this volume. Later, a part of the former laundry in Area 20 was adapted as a storage area for sealed rations. A new western boundary wall was constructed from the north air drift west of the GPO telephone exchange, running south past passenger lift PL1 to the southern perimeter wall just west of emergency exit door 'C', thus completely enclosing areas 8-16, 21 and 22. Most services to the abandoned areas were cut off although minimal ventilation was maintained. Most of these areas had always suffered from the ingress of water and from the high humidity in the quarry and their abandonment reduced considerably the load on the remaining ventilation and air-conditioning plant. A new emergency exit door was constructed in the northern perimeter wall at this time, and access routes were left through the new western perimeter to provide emergency escape routes and to allow access for maintenance and inspection. Access was also required to the power house in Area 19 which continued to function under the new plan.

ALBATROSS

By the early 1980s it was apparent that the Corsham bunker was, in its current state, no longer fit for purpose. In 1982, with maintenance costs running at £600,000 per year and the prospect of major capital costs being incurred as major items of plant became due for replacement, a feasibility study and subsequent report, referred to as 'Project ALBATROSS', was prepared outlining the future of CHANTICLEER over the following twenty-five years.

Little or no material progress was made until September 1988 (by which time the code-name of the headquarters had changed yet again to PERIPHERAL), when the PSA was requested by the Cabinet Office to carry out a pre-design study into the provision of a protected enclave within the existing infrastructure at Spring Quarry. The study was to be completed by May 1989. The terms of reference were similar to that of the earlier feasibility study of 1982 but also included the option of abandoning the site completely if an economically viable solution could not be found. It was explained by Colonel Milton, chairman of the Cabinet Office Central Government in War Planning Team, that, although the area of Spring Quarry designated for use as a central government bunker had reduced considerably since the 1960s the cost of maintenance had continued to rise, many of the facilities were clearly obsolete and much of the original equipment needed replacement. A decision, he

said, was clearly needed on the future of PERIPHERAL and to that end three outline proposals were made:

- That a fully engineered refurbishment of the minimum necessary area should be completed in order to provide an operationally ready facility.
- That the same minimum area should be refurbished but not fitted out until its requirement seemed imminent, and that it should be then in a position to be brought to operational readiness within twenty-eight days.
- That the site should be completely abandoned.

The second option was quickly discounted as it was calculated that the financial benefit would be minimal and that the risk of being unable to source essential equipment during the twenty-eight day readiness period was too great. It had been hoped that this scheme would have required only minimal care and maintenance costs while inactive. The point was raised, however, that should the twenty-eight-day readiness option be adopted then the movement to site and installation of equipment would be undertaken during a time of heightened tension and would go unnoticed as it would be part of a nationwide pattern of increased activity.

Abandonment, it was thought, would cost approximately £750,000 and would take about twelve months to implement. The greater part of the cost would arise from redundancy payments to approximately forty-five permanent maintenance staff, emptying and degassing fuel tanks and making alterations to various service installations shared with the adjacent Admiralty stores depot. After a brief discussion, the Property Services Agency proposed a fourth option of going ahead with the fully engineered, fully fitted-out scheme, but utilising as much as possible of the existing mechanical and electrical plant and equipment. Although reservations were voiced, this proposal appears to have been the most favoured option on a number of grounds, which will be explained in detail below.

The Cabinet Office requirement was for an enclave to house a staff of no more than 1,000 people that was radiation, gas and biohazard-proof and capable of surviving conventional bombing and the effects of all but a direct nuclear burst. Protection was also required against 'unconventional forms of attack', which were not expanded upon in the design brief but presumably included assault by Soviet Spetsnaz Special Force units, home-grown terrorists groups or perhaps by the disaffected proletariat. The facility should also be protected against electro-magnetic pulse (EMP). This was a problem the magnitude of which it was difficult to assess, for until

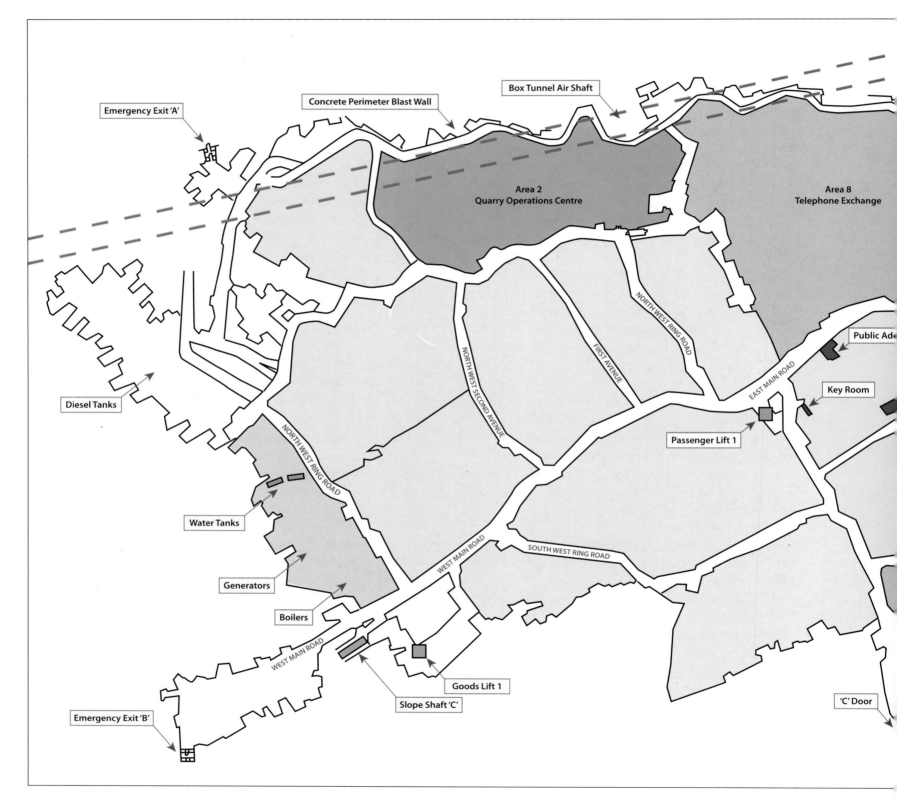

Emergency Exit 'A'

Concrete Perimeter Blast Wall

Box Tunnel Air Shaft

Area 2
Quarry Operations Centre

Area 8
Telephone Exchange

NORTH WEST RING ROAD

Public Ad...

Diesel Tanks

NORTH WEST SECOND AVENUE

FIRST AVENUE

EAST MAIN ROAD

Key Room

Passenger Lift 1

Water Tanks

NORTH WEST RING ROAD

Generators

WEST MAIN ROAD

SOUTH WEST RING ROAD

Boilers

WEST MAIN ROAD

Goods Lift 1

Slope Shaft 'C'

'C' Door

Emergency Exit 'B'

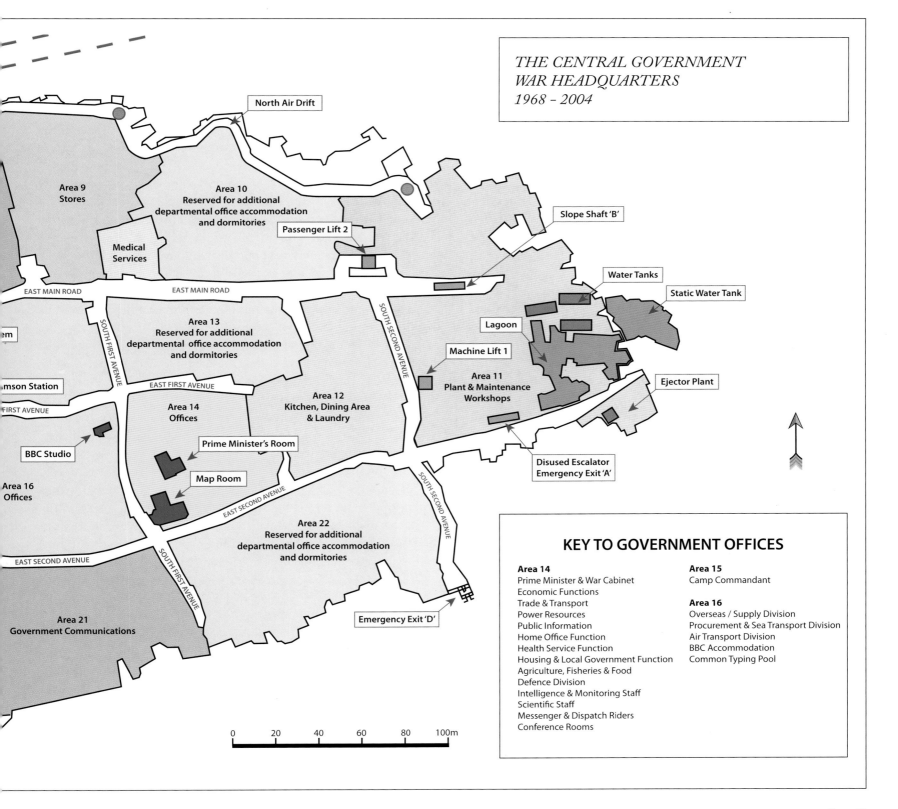

North Air Drift

THE CENTRAL GOVERNMENT
WAR HEADQUARTERS
1968 – 2004

Area 9
Stores

Area 10
Reserved for additional
departmental office accommodation
and dormitories

Passenger Lift 2

Slope Shaft 'B'

Medical
Services

Water Tanks

Static Water Tank

EAST MAIN ROAD   EAST MAIN ROAD

em

Area 13
Reserved for additional
departmental office accommodation
and dormitories

Lagoon

Machine Lift 1

Ejector Plant

SOUTH SECOND AVENUE

SOUTH FIRST AVENUE

mson Station

EAST FIRST AVENUE

Area 12
Kitchen, Dining Area
& Laundry

Area 11
Plant & Maintenance
Workshops

FIRST AVENUE

Area 14
Offices

BBC Studio

Prime Minister's Room

Map Room

Disused Escalator
Emergency Exit 'A'

Area 16
Offices

EAST SECOND AVENUE

SOUTH FIRST AVENUE

SOUTH SECOND AVENUE

Area 22
Reserved for additional
departmental office accommodation
and dormitories

EAST SECOND AVENUE

Area 21
Government Communications

Emergency Exit 'D'

0   20   40   60   80   100m

KEY TO GOVERNMENT OFFICES

Area 14
Prime Minister & War Cabinet
Economic Functions
Trade & Transport
Power Resources
Public Information
Home Office Function
Health Service Function
Housing & Local Government Function
Agriculture, Fisheries & Food
Defence Division
Intelligence & Monitoring Staff
Scientific Staff
Messenger & Dispatch Riders
Conference Rooms

Area 15
Camp Commandant

Area 16
Overseas / Supply Division
Procurement & Sea Transport Division
Air Transport Division
BBC Accommodation
Common Typing Pool

it had actually been experienced it could not be measured. It was thought, however, that the thirty metres of overlying rock and earth would not provide adequate shielding. Representatives from British Telecom suggested that all their equipment could be housed within a floor area of 1,600 square feet and could be contained within two small or one large Faraday cage. Similarly, the BBC suggested that its equipment could be contained in similar housings manufactured by the Belling Lee Company, and could be contained within three rooms or chambers each approximately fifteen feet square. British Telecom were asked to investigate the availability of EMP resilient telephone and teleprinter equipment, including the TREND teleprinters currently in service with the armed forces and about which there were questions regarding their vulnerability.

It was required that the completed headquarters should be self-sufficient for a minimum period of sixty days post-strike and that within that period it should be capable of operating in a sealed, closed-down condition for up to seven days. An insight into the process by which government would be transferred to Corsham in the 1990s can be gleaned from the fact that it was also specified that the facility should be capable of operation covertly for up to thirty days pre-strike. This could be achieved, it was thought, because during that time essential services such as water and electricity would still be available to the site via conventional peacetime sources, and that movement of the relatively small numbers of personnel would be disguised amongst the general intensification of military and government activity in the weeks leading up to war.

An important element of the planning team's terms of reference was that the final design brief should be for a facility that had a life cycle of twenty-five years meaning, in effect, that no further capital expenditure should be required on the infrastructure or major plant components during that period.

Plant & equipment

Much of the existing plant, including the generators, ventilation fans and air-conditioning equipment was relatively simple in design and did not employ solid-state electronics in their control systems and were thus not particularly vulnerable to EMP. It was noted, however, that the ventilation fans dated from the factory era and were more than forty years old and perhaps coming to the end of their useful lives. The four Mirrlees generator sets had been thoroughly overhauled in 1989 and were in excellent order, although it was stated that spare

parts would only be available until 1995, which clearly did not meet the twenty-five year life-cycle criteria. There were other problems too: at Corsham it was found that even when running under test on partial load the engines had a tendency to overheat. More seriously, it was revealed that similar engines installed in British Railways Class 31 locomotives had shown early signs of metal fatigue in the fabricated engine housings and cylinder columns and had been removed and replaced by English Electric type 12SV power units as early as 1964. The Mirrlees locomotive engines were subsequently returned to the factory, reconditioned and sold for less demanding roles such as trawler power plants and other marine applications.

The two Sulzer air-conditioning units, which were now twenty-one years old, were inefficient and increasingly prone to breakdown. Spare parts were no longer available from the manufacturer but it was thought that the PSA could source such components from third-party engineering firms and that in this way the plant could be kept functioning for a further five or ten years.

A review of the communications equipment in Area 8, prepared by British Telecom, revealed that the majority of the apparatus was obsolete and that certain components, including the VF terminal equipment and the Teleprinter Automatic Switching (TAS) installation, had ceased to be operational many years earlier. The forty-position manual sleeve-control switchboard, although maintained by a local BT staff, carried no live or exercise traffic and it was feared that the humidity in the area, which had been allowed to rise in recent years, had had a detrimental effect upon the internal wiring. Interestingly, the BT report states that at the time of inspection in 1982 the switchboards were already forty years old, which suggests that at least some of them may have been sourced from the original factory installation previously housed in Area 1.

The 1,600-line Strowger electro-mechanical exchange seemed in good order, but BT warned that this equipment, too, would be obsolete by the mid-1990s and that staff expertise in its maintenance would become minimal. It was recommended that the existing racks should remain for five or ten years after which consideration should be given to replacing it with a packaged Private Automatic Branch Exchange (PABX) system. Within Area 8 British Telecom maintained a repeater station and transmission equipment which formed part of the peacetime network and it was intended that this would be replaced as part of that organisation's continuous maintenance scheme so there would be no difficulty in securing the viability of the main network outlets for the foreseeable future.

Initially it was thought that because of the high cost of relocation, the communications equipment currently housed in Area 21 and the BBC monitoring equipment in Area 14, room 73, would remain in situ. Later, as we shall see, that plan was altered.

Space requirements

Several options for the proposed redevelopment were explored, each utilising progressively less of the total available space. In the interests of economy in both building costs and subsequent operating costs it was decided that the proposed new facility should be contained within the smallest possible physical footprint and, indeed, the brief was generally described in documents of the time as the 'minimum area scheme'. A working area of five square metres per person was allowed for a maximum staff of 1,000 personnel working a two shift system, with a further 250 square metres allocated for storage areas, briefing and conference rooms and 500 square metres for dining facilities. Even after further space had been allocated for toilets, dormitories, a small kitchen, sick bay and laundry it was calculated that the whole requirement could be contained within a new perimeter wall enclosing areas 8 to 11. The number of personnel allocated to the proposed post-ALBATROSS PERIPHERAL raised questions at the Cabinet Office. Colonel Milton, chairman of the ALBATROSS planning team, when asked whether 'in particular, is the requirement for 1,000 people still valid? Could the site not have a credible role with facilities for only 500 or 750?' replied that:

> '1,000 is the agreed figure from the past; hence no authorisation for modification need be sought and so waste more time. I do not know whether a reduction of requirement to 500 or 700 lessens the credibility of the role; the figure of 1,000 has a mystical quality of great size in many people's minds which might be lacking with any smaller figure.'

All communications equipment would be housed within the northern half of Area 8 while the southern half would contain all the administrative offices, mostly to open-plan designs. Area 9 was initially designated for dormitories (ten single VIP bedrooms, small dormitories with twenty-four single-occupancy beds for senior staff and large dormitories with hot-bedding bunks for 850 male and 120 female staff), and Area 10 for dining and rest rooms, kitchen and sick bay. Later, it was agreed that the roles of these two areas could be reversed if required. The function of Area 11 would remain largely unchanged.

The scheme in outline

The outline plan that evolved from Project ALBATROSS envisaged an emergency headquarters very different in character from the concepts first espoused in the SUBTERFUGE scheme of the late 1950s. Gone were the references to conditions inside the bunker being 'austere and crowded' with 'staff of all grades having to perform unfamiliar and possibly uncongenial tasks under great stress.' Instead, by the 1980s the working environment as described in the ALBATROSS study would be:

> '... busy, animated, but not laboured (in the manual sense). It would therefore require good office standards of lighting, a fresh but warm atmosphere and other measures taken to assist in the psychological well-being of the personnel who could be retained in the complex for months on end. (Sixty days self-sufficiency is the minimum brief requirement.) Frequent high-level meetings would take place in a secure conference room itself having provision for telephone, data access via terminals and freedom from eavesdropping.

> 'Area 9 would be the general feeding, relaxation and recreation area of the complex. Stress will play a part in regulating the efficiency of this complex and careful provision of videos, exercise and quiet areas would have been made available in this respect. The medical centre is seen as a refuge for psychological relief as well as care for various categories of serious illnesses.

> 'The overall picture is therefore one of a substantial open area with relatively quiet working activities. The emphasis, as far as design is concerned, should therefore be to provide a facility which is quiet and pleasantly fitted-out in working area, but with variations in colour, fittings and noise to intelligently enliven the environment of those carrying out such important duties.'

Much was made, too, of the value of green plants, not just on account of their therapeutic value but also because of their ability to absorb carbon dioxide from the atmosphere and also the harmful chemicals emitted by modern office furniture including formaldehyde, benzene and other hydrocarbons. It was even suggested that facilities should be provided to propagate certain species of plants underground under artificial illumination.

It was intended that entry to the bunker would be via passenger lift PL2 only, and that new hardened head-works, including a security and decontamination unit, would be built above it. A second decontamination unit would be provided at the bottom of the

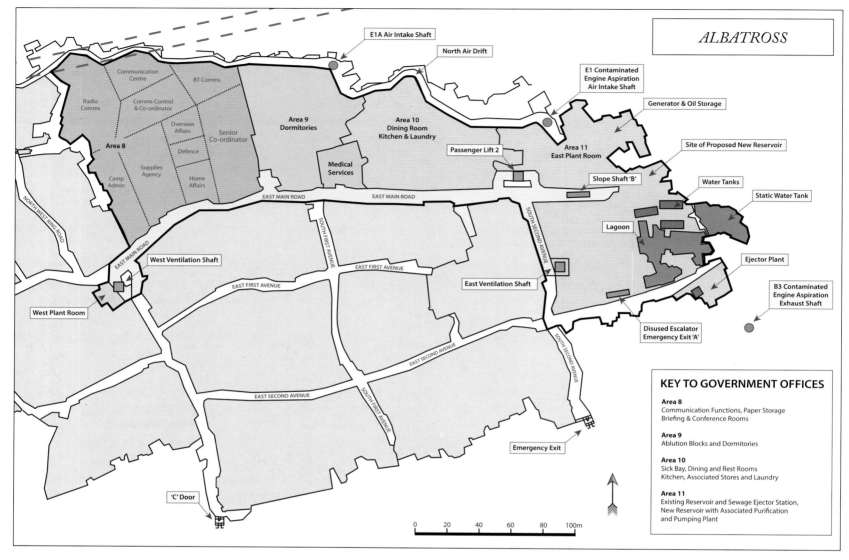

escalator in shaft 'C', which would be immobilised as an emergency exit staircase, and another decontamination unit adjacent to an air-locked emergency exit into the surrounding quarries.

The passenger lift in shaft PL1 would be removed, the head-works hardened and the shaft adapted as part of the ventilation system. The area around the shaft bottom, together with a section of Area 18, would be enclosed by new concrete walls and would serve as the west end service plant room. A similar plant room would be established near shaft E1 in Area 11 to serve the east end of the site. There was much debate as to what equipment would be fitted in these areas although it was agreed that each would include two standby generators rated at approximately two megawatts and each

would have identical air-conditioning units, heat exchangers and electrostatic Nuclear, Biological and Chemical (NBC) filtration units. Two detailed alternatives were proposed, one which envisaged the provision of new equipment of the most modern designs currently available whilst the other, which found increasing favour, involved the retention of the existing generators, fans and air-treatment plants but moving them to the new locations. The advantages of the latter plan were that, due to the inevitable lead time in specifying and acquiring new plant, the interruption to the service availability of the site would be minimised, initial capital expenditure would be deferred and, due to the absence of sophisticated electronic control circuitry, the plant would be unaffected by EMP. The advantage, as stated in the report, would be that 'plant installed in the future can be selected as state-of-the-art.'

Much attention was paid to the detail design of these plant rooms and their associated airways. Although, if the existing equipment was initially reused, EMP would not be a major issue, it was realised that its eventual replacement would create a problem. To forestall this, it was planned that the whole of each plant room should be encased in a substantial Faraday cage constructed of continuously-welded 33mm steel plate supported by an external steel-girder framework, the whole bonded to a matrix of copper earth straps buried in the ground above. This feature alone was expected to add in excess of £1,000,000 to the cost of the project.

British Telecom were asked to quote for a completely new communications facility, housed in protective enclosures as detailed above and located in the area currently occupied by the existing line transmission and repeater station. The installation cost for the new facility was estimated at £670,000 and the annual rental charge at £131,000. Twenty exchange lines were required, along with a number of Private Wire circuits to the following locations:

- British Telecom Emergency Manual Switching System centres at Worcester, Reading and Merthyr Tydfil. These represented, essentially, BT's 'last-ditch' switching system which they would fall back upon if the greater part of the automatic system were put out of action. Use of this system would allow limited communication between the central government nucleus, the Regional Headquarters and civil facilities that were not otherwise provided with links to the emergency communications network.
- Four strategically selected Regional Government Headquarters: RGHQ 7.1 at Chilmark in the southwest, 9.2 at Drakelow in the Midlands, 4.1 at Shipton in the north and 1.1 at Hertford in the eastern region.
- The RAF / MoD No.6 Signals Unit and RAF Rudloe Manor communications centre located in adjacent underground facilities at Corsham.
- The UKWMO Sector Control Centre at Lansdown near Bath.
- The BBC Emergency Headquarters at Wood Norton.
- The BBC monitoring station at Caversham.
- The NATO Civil Wartime Agencies headquarters at Cambridge.
- The BT Defence Network control centre at Oswestry and standby site at Shepton Mallet. The auto-manual trunk

telephone exchange at Shepton Mallet, which was extended in 1953 and again in the 1960s, probably provided an alternative Corsham-Bristol cable route but, more importantly, provided a junction point to the Home Office radio transmission station at Cranmore Tower on a hilltop overlooking the town. Cranmore Tower was a hub in the MOULD radio network, which was itself aligned to the geographical boundaries of the regional government areas. Cranmore had links to sites on the Region 7.1 (Chilmark) sub-net and the 7.2 (Bolt Head) sub-net, as well as the Somerset County radio network.
- The RAF communications centre at Boddington.
- The USAF communications centre at Croughton.
- Cold Blow ACE high communications facility.
- Swingate RAF communications link to German stations.
- Henlow Defence Communication Services facility.
- Forest Moor Royal Navy high frequency communications centre.
- Fort Southwick Royal Navy communications centre.
- HM Government Communications Centre (HMGCC) at Hanslope Park, home to the UK Foreign & Commonwealth Office research centre responsible, inter-alia, for the development of communications and enciphering apparatus.
- Fylingdales ballistic missile early warning station in north Yorkshire.
- Northwood NATO HQ and PJHQ of the RN Fleet Commander.
- Oakhanger ground-station for UK military communications satellites.
- Pitrivie Castle, NATO North Atlantic Headquarters and Air and Naval Force Commander North Atlantic.
- St. Mawgan Coastal Command HQ and Nimrod base.
- Rugby radio station. Covering a 1,600-acre site, Rugby Radio was the largest radio transmission station in the world, handling the majority of the United Kingdom's international radio-telephone traffic. The site also housed strategically important Admiralty Very Low Frequency (VLF) transmission equipment, used to communicate with submarines at sea.
- Somerton radio station in Somerset. This site was the principal receiving station for Rugby.

The whole of the existing electro-mechanical exchange racks, transmission equipment, power plant and manual switchboards from Area 8, together with the teleprinters and associated transmission equipment in Area 21, would become surplus to requirements, and its ultimate disposal a problem. Apart from cost considerations, it was feared that the transportation of so much redundant equipment away from Corsham might be observed by people of dubious intent, and thus the PERIPHERAL secret would be blown. To avoid this possibility, the Cabinet Office notified British Telecom that:

> 'If normal scrap disposal is not possible unwanted BT equipment could be dumped in abandoned areas. It should be dispersed in several abandoned areas so that the totality of equipment would not be apparent to an unauthorised observer. Consideration should be given to burying it in disused areas and covering it with rubble.'

EYEGLASS & the end of PERIPHERAL

No progress, however, was made towards implementing the ALBATROSS scheme and towards the end of 1990 it seemed as though the end of PERIPHERAL was in sight. In November discussions were in hand regarding the transfer of custody of the site to the Ministry of Defence, which already occupied other areas of quarry contiguous with the Spring Quarry complex, for use as a possible location for the proposed Defence Fixed Telecommunications System (DFTS) network management system. The DFTS, following its inauguration in 1995, replaced nineteen existing military communications networks with one integrated service-wide system. The principal motive for the Property Services Agency, who looked after the Spring Quarry complex on behalf of the Cabinet Office, was to offload the £500,000 per year maintenance costs onto the MoD, and the latter had suspicions that this might be the case. A spokesman for the MoD involved in the negotiations noted to his superior 'I hope we are not taking on a liability we shall come to regret, and that the normal proprieties are observed. This is of course especially important if the transfer is not to attract unwelcome attention.'

The transfer went ahead in March 1991 although the Cabinet Office remained, as tenants of the MoD, in possession of areas 12-16 and Area 21. The reason for this residual interest is difficult to unravel but the scanty evidence available indicates that it appears to have concerned a communication facility within Area 21, maintained for the potential use of the Foreign and Commonwealth Office (FCO). Some years earlier there had been conversations between the Cabinet

Office, the GPO and the BBC over the establishment of a last-ditch link between the Corsham bunker and FCO posts in Australia that would remain viable if all conventional communications were lost. A few months later, in October 1991, a somewhat mysterious memo from the Cabinet Office advised that work on EYEGLASS in PERIPHERAL should be slowed down, and that the FCO could withdraw their facilities if they wished but, 'because of the long lead-time to produce equipment, you should continue to earmark suitable radio and cryptographic equipment to communicate with Leading Posts.' The writer went on to stress that 'this letter refers to PERIPHERAL arrangements only. Other plans remain unchanged at present.' The following February, subsequent to a discussion at a meeting of the Cabinet Office Machinery of Government in War Committee regarding the possible installation of a fibre-optic cable into the EYEGLASS facility, it was even more mysteriously minuted that 'no committee member felt it necessary to comment on a recommendation for the continued existence of EYEGLASS in a decoy role, at the minimal cost of £25,000 per year.'

Whatever its role, EYEGLASS remained at PERIPHERAL until almost the end of the decade. In June 1999, however, it was reported that the condition of the site had deteriorated so badly that PERIPHERAL was no longer viable. Commenting on their facility at Corsham, a representative of the Cabinet Office Defence and Overseas Affairs Secretariat stated that there were two BBC elements in EYEGLASS: a broadcasting studio and a monitoring studio, both provided with two communications circuits, one being a standard telephone line and the other a four-wire music-quality broadcasting line. Both were direct links from the BBC monitoring station at Caversham to their emergency war headquarters at Wood Norton, but were routed through PERIPHERAL so could be broken into for PERIPHERAL (and hence EYEGLASS) use if it was activated. It was stated that as the PERIPHERAL telephone exchange was no longer operational the telephone line was now redundant and the Cabinet Office had no objection to the BBC removing its residual equipment. Shortly afterwards, just before the decision was finally taken to declassify the site in 2004, items of equipment were removed from the communications centre under conditions of great secrecy. There is currently no indication what this might have been, nor is there likely to be in the foreseeable future, but it is speculated that it included enciphering apparatus subsequently returned to Hanslope Park.

Chapter 3

ENTRANCES & EXITS

Above: Aerial view of Westwells Road at Corsham showing the surface features of the CGWHQ bunker.

Right: The surface head-works of Goods Lift GL1. The massive concrete structure on top of the earthen mound contains the lift motor-room while the earth embankments both camouflage and give added protection to the entrance vestibule and lobby below. Compare this image with the photograph on *page 22* which shows the same structure in its wartime factory configuration, without earth protection and surrounded by storage sheds.

Above: The heavily protected surface entrance to Passenger Lift PL1.
Below: One of the pair of PL1 lift cages, semi-derelict and abandoned at the bottom of the lift shaft.
Right: The underground entrance vestibule of Passenger Lift PL1, virtually unchanged in appearance from its wartime factory days.

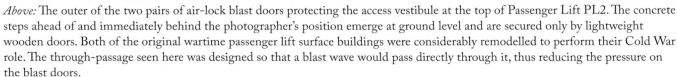

Above: The outer of the two pairs of air-lock blast doors protecting the access vestibule at the top of Passenger Lift PL2. The concrete steps ahead of and immediately behind the photographer's position emerge at ground level and are secured only by lightweight wooden doors. Both of the original wartime passenger lift surface buildings were considerably remodelled to perform their Cold War role. The through-passage seen here was designed so that a blast wave would pass directly through it, thus reducing the pressure on the blast doors.

Right: One of the two PL2 lift cars, stationary at the upper landing, looking out through the vestibule and the openings of the two air-lock doors to the access passage beyond.

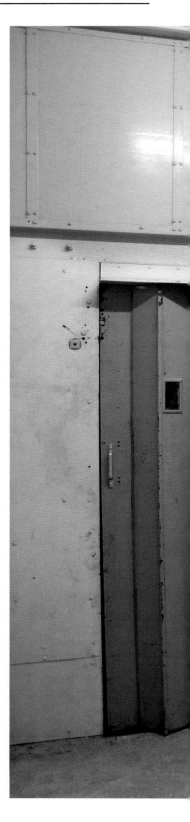

Above: The lower lift landing of PL2 at quarry floor level. Both sets of passenger lifts were double-sided allowing personnel to embark and disembark expeditiously. While of little importance to the functioning of the CGWHQ, it was vitally importance during the Second World War when up to six thousand workers would transfer to and from the surface at each shift change. This view shows the rear access passage with a pair of call-handles mounted on a central pillar.

Left: The original bronze Otis lift controller in lift car No.4.

Right: The front entrance to Passenger Lift PL2. Originally these lifts were fitted with open, expanding lattice gates, but in the 1960s they were replaced by the folding gates seen here.

Left: The modest, earth-mounded entrance to the west escalator shaft gives little indication of what lays within.

Right: None of the escalators requisitioned from St. Paul's and Holborn tube stations were long enough to span the entire length of the quarry incline shafts, so at the west end two units were installed end-on-end with their junction at a spectacular underground intermediate landing. This view shows the shorter, upper flight ascending to the surface. The inclined concrete structure to the left supports a winch-operated goods haulage system.

Below: This view is taken from the intermediate landing towards the lower escalator incline.

Above: The base of the west escalator at quarry floor level. Now partially dismantled and in very poor condition, it has been disused since the late 1960s. The moving handrails and associated components have been removed, suggesting that there was perhaps a plan to adapt it, like the east escalator, as a fixed emergency stairway, but this has never been completed. Instead, the flight of broad concrete steps to the right provides an adequate escape route to the surface.

Opposite: A view looking down the lower flight of the west escalator. Behind the wall to the left is a flight of stairs, used as an emergency exit and beyond the right-hand wall is the inclined haulageway described on the previous page.

Left: Part of the drive mechanism for the west escalator. Although, to the user, escalators appear quite simple devices, they are in fact very complex machines. Most of the mechanism, however, is hidden from sight below floor level.

Below left: The centrifugal overspeed governor which prevented the escalator descending too quickly. When the machine is running the two balls at the top of the device rotate about the central spindle; the faster they rotate the further they move outwards under centrifugal force. Due to the pivoted linkage seen in this photograph, the outwards movement of the rotating balls raises the collar and operates a control mechanism.

Below right: A 20-position hydrostatic displacement lubricator which supplied a constant, metered amount of oil to the various bearings and other moving components in the escalator drive system.

Left: The drive motor and gear box for the upper west end escalator.

Below left: Until very recently the provenance of the Corsham escalators was an enigma. Contradictory documents discovered in the National Archives suggested two alternative origins for the escalators. The first suggested that they were installed in their respective underground stations in the 1930s and had been requisitioned and later removed for use at Corsham; the other that they were still under construction in the Otis factory when they were requisitioned and were redirected to Corsham. The lubrication identification plate, seen in this photograph, bears the inscription 'Holborn Esc. No.4' which proves conclusively that the escalator had been removed from the stations rather than diverted from the factory.

Below right: This scale indicates the amount of wear in the escalator tread rollers and allows accurate adjustments to be made.

Above: Just as at the west end, the escalator requisitioned for the east end of the quarry was too short to reach the surface, but here a different solution was found. At this location the escalator terminates in a chamber approximately twenty feet below ground level from where access to the surface continues in the form of a spiral staircase, the bottom of which can be seen in the background.

Opposite: By the early 1970s both escalators had become unserviceable due to a prolonged lack of maintenance. Whilst the west end unit was abandoned, the east end escalator was secured in position, the moving handrails removed and a modern fixed handrail attached to the guide rails to form a fixed emergency stairway.

Above: The bottom of the east escalator at quarry floor level, showing the neat arrangement of handrails added when it was converted into a pedestrian emergency exit route.

Chapter 4

THE AREAS

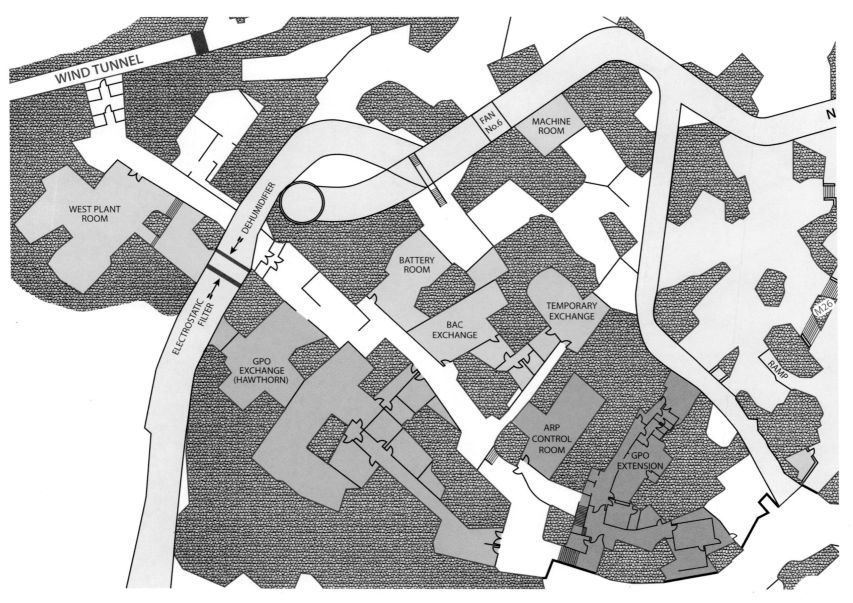

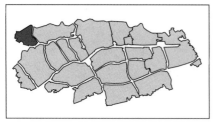

Area 1 is largely disused and is mainly taken up by the location of the former GPO underground 'Hawthorn' telephone exchange and the Bristol Aeroplane Company's wartime factory internal exchange. The GPO extension exchange, to the east of the area, appears to have been fitted out in the late 1950s and included male and female dormitories and welfare facilities. It is probable that this provided temporary services for SUBTERFUGE, utilising redundant apparatus from the Hawthorn exchange, while the new 'Woodlands' facility was under construction in Area 8.

Left: Little now remains of the long-abandoned wartime telephone exchange other than a few rotting doors.

Below right: Forty years ago, cavers exploring the labyrinth of abandoned stone workings at Box found their way, by hacking through coiled barbed-wire, into a passageway now commonly known as the 'Wind Tunnel'. At the end of the tunnel they discovered this imposing and immovable steel door set into a concrete wall. No one was sure what it was all about but soon, with some prescience, someone wrote on it in chalk the line from the Bob Dylan's song *Subterranean Homesick Blues*: 'Look out kid, they keep it all hid.' What they had found was one of the emergency exits from the Corsham CGWHQ. The exit route was intended to go through the old workings to a new vertical shaft in Box Fields, but the planned spiral stairway was never installed and work on reinforcing the route was abandoned.

Below left: The portal of the inside blast door of the air-lock leading to the emergency exit door into the Wind Tunnel.

Left: The wartime factory ventilation system consisted of a number of vertical inlet shafts through which fresh air was drawn, then heated and circulated around the factory via large underground ducts with strategically placed outlets throughout the site. Foul air was drawn from the factory via ceiling-level trunking connected to the north air drift and discharged to the surface by fans in vertical exhaust shafts. The existing infrastructure was adapted to provide a recirculatory ventilation system for the CGWHQ. The inlet shafts were sealed and air continuously circulated within the headquarters, with small quantities of fresh make-up air admitted when required from the old workings that comprised the surrounding east and west lungs. This view, taken from the base of the now sealed B1 inlet shaft, shows the start of the west end underground air ducts. The roof of this duct has been cut through to enable partially vitiated air from the north air drift to be drawn back into the system for recirculation.

Left: This view, taken near the west end of the north air drift, shows the steel hangers upon which telephone cables from the old GPO telephone exchange were supported. The cables would have entered the inclined tubes in the floor near the right-hand wall which fed them beneath the perimeter wall and into the Wind Tunnel. The cables were supported on brackets for the length of the Wind Tunnel from where they continued in a duct beneath the floor of the old quarry workings to emerge at Clift Works entrance. There on the A4 trunk road, they joined into the main GPO cable network.

Below right: When the underground factory was constructed early in the Second World War, it was assumed that the Luftwaffe would deploy chemical weapons against the United Kingdom from an early stage. To reduce the risk of mustard gas being drawn into the factory's ventilation system, remotely controlled butterfly valves, like the example shown here, were incorporated in the air ducts to rapidly stop the circulation of contaminated air.

Opposite below left: Exterior view of No.6 ventilation fan showing the electric motor and belt drive within its safety cage. The red cylinders are lubricators for the fan's main bearings and between them is a pair of thermometers measuring the bearing temperatures.

Opposite below right: The outlet side of No.6 fan, within its brick-lined ventilation duct.

Above: Sulzer air-conditioning units in the west plant room. Under uncontrolled conditions, the temperature underground remains at a constant 8°C and the humidity is normally above 90%, conditions too cold for sustained work. The high humidity, too, would be uncomfortable to work in and would cause the rapid decay of organic materials like paper, or timber, the corrosion of metals, and would have a detrimental effect on delicate electronic equipment.

The continuous through-ventilation employed during the factory era was marginally successful but exorbitantly expensive to operate, did little to reduce humidity during the summer months, and had to be shut down completely if there was any risk of contamination of the incoming air. During the early 1950s a system of refrigerated air-conditioning was successfully installed at two neighbouring quarries used for long-term ammunition storage, and in 1961 it was decided to install an updated form of this equipment in the CGWHQ.

Four sets of Sulzer refrigeration plant were installed, two units in each of two plant rooms, one at the east and one at the west end of the headquarters.

The equipment operates on a similar thermodynamic cycle to a domestic refrigerator: within an enclosed circuit a compressor forces coolant through a condenser into which it releases heat; from the condenser it passes via an expansion valve into an evaporator from which it extracts heat as it expands, returning to the compressor to repeat the cycle. By having cooling water circulate around the condenser a supply of hot water is obtained to heat radiators positioned in the ventilation air-flow. Similarly, water circulating around the evaporator produces a supply of chilled water used to cool incoming air.

Air cooled by chilled water from the evaporator can hold much less moisture than warm air, so at that point the atmospheric moisture drops out. The chilled air then passes through radiators connected to the condenser circuit which raises it to a comfortable temperature. As the warm, dry air circulates it gradually picks up moisture from human respiration and from the surrounding rock strata. Vitiated air eventually returns to the plant via the ventilation ducts and the process is repeated.

Above left: No.1 Sulzer plant in the west plant room. Each unit has a 250 ton refrigeration rating meaning that under perfect conditions it could produce or extract sufficient heat to melt or freeze 250 tons of ice in 24 hours.

Above right: Hot water radiator positioned in the north air drift.

Left: Condense water pipelines in the north air drift supplying the radiator visible in the background. The chilled water pipelines, (seen in the photograph opposite), were insulated and lagged in aluminium foil.

AREA 2
1961-1968 GOVERNMENT DEPARTMENTS

Area 2 is contained within the boundaries of the most northerly of the Bristol Aeroplane Company's four operatives canteens. Many features of its Second World War function still survive, including several fine examples of Olga Lehmann's floor-to-ceiling murals, painted to render the workers' relaxation areas a little less oppressive. During the early years of the CGWHQ office space within this area was allocated to a number of the government departments with the least important roles to play during the immediate survival phase of a nuclear conflict.

KEY TO AREA 2

CUSTOMS & EXCISE
1   All Questions

HER MAJESTY'S STATIONERY OFFICE
2   All Questions

MINISTRY OF WORKS
3   Senior Representatives
13   Other Representatives

BOARD OF TRADE
4   Deputy Secretary
5   Permanent Secretary
6   Under-Secretary, Assistant Secretary, Principal,
     Clerical Officer Secretary
7   Under-Secretary, Assistant Secretary, Principal,
     Clerical Officer Secretary
8   Industrialists
9   Under-Secretary, Assistant Secretary, Principal,
     Clerical Officer Secretary
10   Principal, HEO & Clerical Officer Secretary,
     Private Secretary
11   Principal, HEO & Clerical Officer Secretary,
     Private Secretary

MINISTRY OF PENSIONS & NATIONAL INSURANCE
& NATIONAL ASSISTANCE BOARD
14   Chairman, or Permanent Secretary (or Deputy)
     National Assistance Board
15   Permanent or Deputy Secretary of the Ministry,
     Private Secretary
16   Minister of Pensions & National Insurance
17   Private Secretary, Ministry of Pensions
     & National Insurance & National Assistance Board
18   Message (or signal) Room & Registry,
     Clerical & Typing
19   Administration - Pensions, Insurance
     & National Assistance
     Legal Matters - Pensions, Insurance
     & National Assistance
20   General Policy - Pensions, Insurance
     & National Assistance

HER MAJESTY'S TREASURY, TREASURY
& PARLIAMENTARY COUNSEL
25   Principals & Others
26   Senior Officer
27   Treasury Solicitor
28   Parliamentary Counsel
43,46   Principals & Others
47   Senior Officer

LORD CHANCELLOR'S OFFICE
29   Permanent Secretary
30   Personal Assistant to Permanent Secretary, SEO

OFFICE OF THE MINISTRY FOR SCIENCE
44   Atomic Energy Authority
45   Secretary to Medical Research Council,
     Secretary to Agricultural Research Council,
     Secretary to Scientific & Industrial Research Council

DORMITORIES

UNALLOCATED

Above and below: The west end of Area 2 was designated as open-plan dormitories for junior staff working in the adjoining government offices. The dormitories were established in what had been the dining area of one of the Bristol Aeroplane Company's operatives' canteens, which still retained a number of Olga Lehmann's murals from that period. Each of the factory's canteens were decorated to a particular theme; here the theme is horse racing and country sports.

AREA 2
CIRCA 1970-2004 RAF OPERATIONS CENTRE

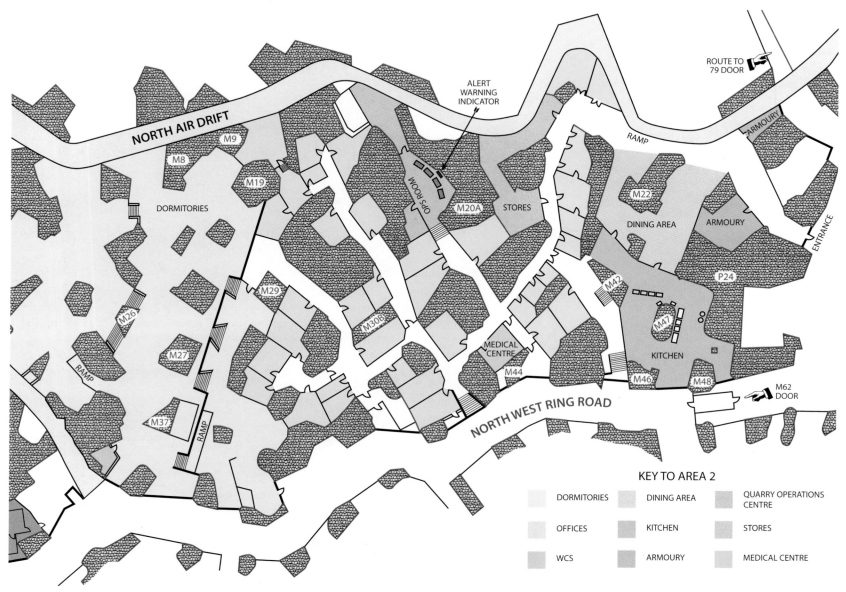

ROUTE TO
79 DOOR

ALERT
WARNING
INDICATOR

NORTH AIR DRIFT

RAMP

ARMOURY

M9

M8

M19

M22

DORMITORIES

OPS ROOM

M20A

STORES

DINING AREA

ARMOURY

ENTRANCE

M29

M42

P24

M26

M30B

M47

M27

MEDICAL
CENTRE

KITCHEN

RAMP

M44

M46

M48

M37

RAMP

M62
DOOR

NORTH WEST RING ROAD

KEY TO AREA 2

DORMITORIES	DINING AREA	QUARRY OPERATIONS CENTRE
OFFICES	KITCHEN	STORES
WCS	ARMOURY	MEDICAL CENTRE

During the early 1970s, following the gradual implementation of the PYTHON scheme, most of the accommodation in the west end of the CGWHQ became redundant. Area 2, selected due to its proximity to their adjacent underground communication centres, was handed over to the RAF and redeveloped as the Quarry Operations Centre (QOC). The principal functions of the QOC were to provide local ground defence for the CGWHQ, supply situation reports on RAF facilities nationwide, and to house the emergency headquarters of the RAF Provost and Security Service.

Above left: When the Quarry Operations Centre was established in the early 1970s all the previous access points to the CGWHQ were sealed off and a new access established from the adjoining RAF communications centre via No.79 door. This photograph shows the new air-lock doors securing the QOC from the access and ventilation passageways beyond.

Above right: A general view of the QOC control room, with Olga Lehmann's 'Wrestlers' mural visible in the background.

Left: This direction sign, near the entrance to the QOC, indicates the range of facilities accommodated there.

Above: The central operations room of the Quarry Operations Centre. The air-conditioning was shut down only a short time before this photograph was taken, yet the deterioration is already quite marked. When operational the walls facing the crescent of desks would have been covered with situation maps. The two wall-mounted monitors showed the views captured by cameras outside doors 79 and 62 on the internal and external approaches to the QOC. Note the attack state board above the desks, shown more clearly on the following page.

Above left and right: The illuminated alert and attack state indicator, positioned prominently in the QOC control centre. From left to right the stencilled panels indicate an increasingly tense external situation; when the lights flashed on behind 'Air Attack Black' and 'Red', then Britain would be under immediate nuclear attack, the state of the nation would be pretty desperate, and all the expense of the CGWHQ would perhaps be justified.

Left: The communications section of the QOC control room with its tiered rows of operators' desks. Once an impressive sight, the high level of humidity in the uncontrolled underground environment has already taken its toll. Although nominally an RAF installation, the QOC was linked into a number of central government communications circuits including the 'Whitehall' teleprinter network.

Left: The QOC was a self-contained unit with a mixed-sex staff of approximately 600 RAF personnel. As well as dormitories it was provided with its own catering and medical facilities. Much of the kitchen equipment was second-hand, recovered from the west kitchen in the CGWHQ following the 1968 reorganisation.

Below left: The bain-maries, or heated serving consoles, were new acquisitions powered by electricity, as those potentially recoverable from the CGWHQ kitchens were steam heated and no steam mains were available in the QOC.

Below right: The QOC was provided with medical facilities on only a limited scale, essentially a single-room First Aid centre.

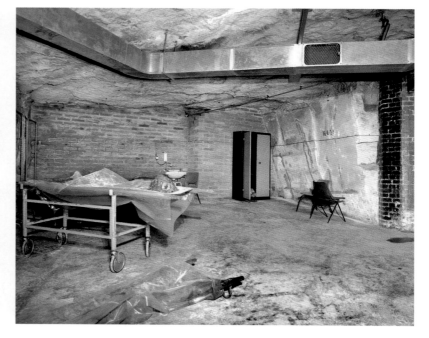

AREAS 3, 4 & 5
DORMITORIES

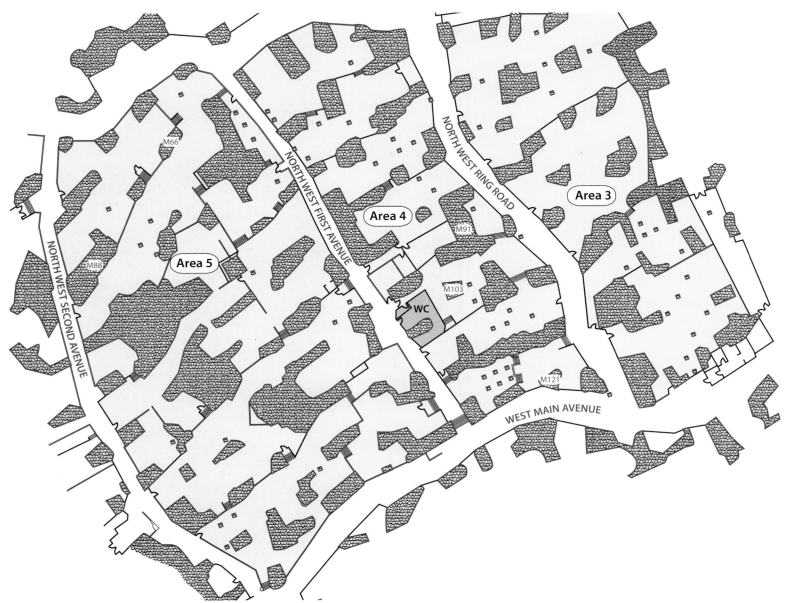

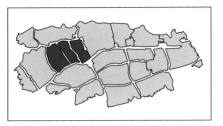

Areas 3, 4 and 5 were reserved as dormitories for lower-ranking civil servants and technical staff working in departments located at the west end of the CGWHQ. Sections of areas 9, 15, 18 and 22 were also designated as dormitory space for staff working in offices in these or adjacent areas. More senior staff, who may have been called upon to work at any hour of the day, were allocated 'Type A' rooms which were combined bedrooms and offices. A small number of Cabinet Ministers were provided with private bedrooms in Area 14.

Opposite: Typical dormitory space within Area 4. Little work was done to prepare these areas for their intended purpose although modern lighting was installed throughout and, as can be seen in this photograph, they were provided with synchronous clocks connected to a central master clock. The CGWHQ public address system was also extended throughout the dormitory areas; a Tannoy loudspeaker is just visible, partially obscured by the light fitting above and to the right of the clock on the right-hand wall.

Above: A rather bleak and oppressive section of Area 5 allocated for dormitory use. Furniture and bedding for areas 3, 4 and 5 was kept in a store-room adjacent to the south-east corner of Area 3 and would have been put in place only when instructions were received to activate the headquarters.

AREAS 6 & 7
CANTEEN, KITCHEN & INDUSTRIAL BAKERY

Serveries

Flour store

Dough machines

Ovens

Water cooling tanks

Generators

Boilers

M54

M73

M92

J56A

J56

M113

NORTH WEST SECOND AVENUE

NORTH WEST RING ROAD

WEST MAIN ROAD

KEY TO AREAS 6, 7 & 19

KITCHEN

DINING AREA

BAKERY

UNUSED

PLANT

Area 6 housed an extensive industrial bakery and Area 7 contained one of the two kitchen and canteen complexes with which the CGWHQ was originally provided. Both areas were abandoned in 1968 as a consequence of the reorganisation of the CGWHQ's function at that time. Most of the bakery equipment survives in-situ, though in poor condition due to the high ambient humidity, but much of the kitchen equipment in Area 7 has been dismantled and either transferred to the QOC catering facility in Area 2 or dumped, for no apparent reason, in adjacent areas.

Above: The W.F. Mason fully automatic bread plant. Capable of producing 1,000 4lb loaves of bread during an eight-hour shift, this machine was installed in the bakery in October 1958 at a cost of £2,096.

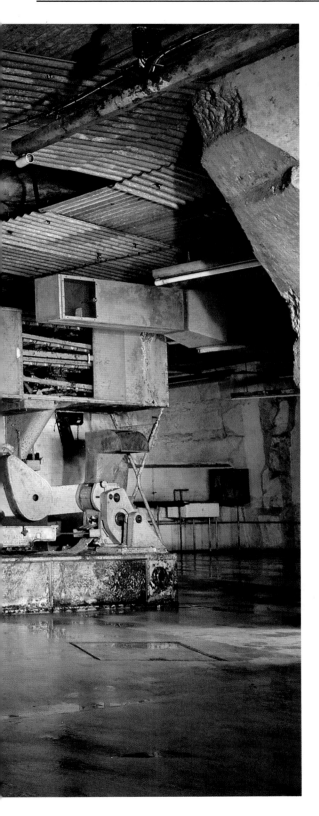

Above: In the background are two double-decker, oil-fired steam-tube bread ovens. The machine in the foreground is an eighty-quart cake mixer.

Left: Panoramic view of the bakery with the ovens in the background, bread machine to the right and warming cupboards, dough trolleys and racks of baking tins lining the left-hand passageway.

Below: Sacks of flour from the stores on the left were tipped into the sieve and dispenser ready for transfer into the bowl of the kneading machine, seen on the right of this picture.

Opposite: Steam-heated boiling pans in the abandoned west kitchen. The ovens seen above are positioned behind the central pillar in this photograph. One of the three deep-fat fryers in this area is just visible behind pillar number M92.

Above: A pair of steam-heated ovens in the west kitchen. A third oven has been removed along with much of the other equipment from this kitchen. It was intended that this would be reinstalled in the QOC catering area but this plan was abandoned when it was realised there were no convenient steam mains nearby.

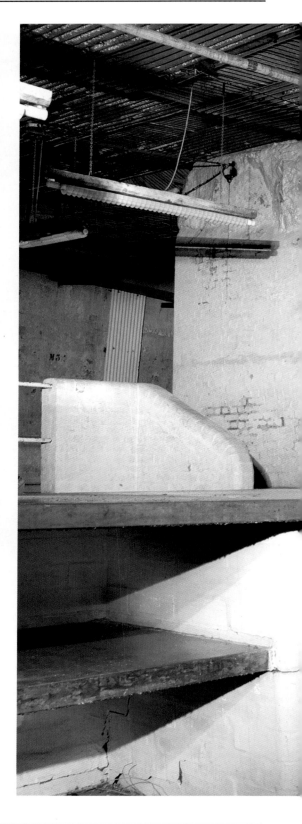

Above: Abandoned catering equipment dumped in a store-room in the northwest corner of the kitchen. Amongst other items can be seen two meat slicers, three tea urns, two steam boiling pans and two or three derelict bain-maries. It is probable that all of this was dismantled with the intention of transferring it to the QOC kitchen some time after 1968, but that this was abandoned when it was decided to use all-electric appliances there. There may, however, have been a wider and unrecorded agenda because other equipment from the west kitchen, including at least two electric deep-fat fryers, was also dismantled, only to be later dumped in the nearby laundry facility.

Right: The depleted remains of the north servery. Several bain-maries and hotplates have been removed from this area, which is now suffering badly from the high humidity and ingress of seepage water. The centrally placed kitchen was surrounded by three serveries similar to this, with a separate, small tea-bar adjacent to the eastern end of the servery seen in this photograph.

BOX TUNNEL

NORTH AIR DRIFT

BOX TUNNEL

BOX TUNNEL

RECTIFIER ROOM

POWER ROOM

TRANSMISSION & REPEATER STATION

TELEGRAPH AUTO

MAIN DISTRIBUTION FRAME

BATTERY ROOM

AUTOMATIC TELEPHONE EXCHANGE

BATTERY CHARGERS

REST ROOM

SPARE ROOM

FEMALE WELFARE

WC

OLD IRON STORE

MANUAL SWITCH ROOM

MANUAL SWITCH ROOM

SUB STN

STORAGE

NORTH WEST RING ROAD

RAMP

EAST MAIN ROAD

Area 8 was the realm of the General Post Office and housed a GPO (subsequently BT) domestic trunk exchange, an international exchange, the CGWHQ internal automatic exchange, an automatic telegraph exchange, a transmission and repeater station and all the necessary power plant to maintain it in operation. Offices for other GPO functions including postal, radio and broadcasting services, as well as the road services and engineering departments, were also accommodated within this area. Floors in the communications areas are colour coded according to function and this is reflected in the plan above.

KEY TO AREA 8

COMMON SERVICES
1,28 Messengers
29,30 Registry
62 Typists (Teleprinter Room)

RADIO SERVICES DEPARTMENT
2 Frequency Plans above 30 mc/s
4 Frequency Plans below 30 mc/s
6 Wireless Telegraph Ship-to-Shore
Communications
7 Officer-in-Charge
8 Inspector of Wireless Telegraphy
9 Accountant-General's Department
11 Assistant Secretary
12 Director

UNALLOCATED
5, 10, 15

EXTERNAL TELECOMMUNICATIONS EXECUTIVE
13 Director
14 Deputy Director
31 Engineering: Lines & Telephones
32 Traffic: Telephones & Telegraphs
36 Engineering: Telegraphs
37 Engineering: Radio
38 Officer-in-Charge

POSTAL SERVICES DEPARTMENT
16 Chief Inspector
18 Director
33 Principal (Home Mails) & Senior Inspector
(Home Mails)
34 Principal (Overseas Mails), Senior Inspector
(Overseas Mails)
35 Principal (General Assistance on Postal Matters)

ENGINEERING DEPARTMENT
17 Engineering Officer
19 Engineering Officer
21 Deputy Engineer-in-Chief
22 Private Secretary
49 Radio Planning & Provision Branch:
Radio above 30 mc/s
50 Radio Planning & Provision Branch:
Officer-in-Charge
51 Telecommunications Services Intelligence:
Officer-in-Charge
51 Emergency Equipment Group: Drawing Office
52 Main Lines: Officer-in-Charge
53 Main Lines: Deputy
54 Circuit Provision Group: Officer-in-Charge,
Public circuits, BBC, AM, USAF, ROC,
HO, MOT, MOA
54 Radio Planning & Provision Branch:
Radio below 30 mc/s
55 Circuit Provision Group: CEGB, Nationalised
Undertakings, Public Utilities, Press,
Admiralty, WO, FO, GCHQ, DTN, PO Admin,
Circuit Advice Control, Card Records,
Line Plant Records etc

55 Emergency Equipment Group: Typing
56 Lines Information Group (Fault Control):
Officer-in-Charge
56 Emergency Equipment Group: Officer-in-Charge
56 Submarine Branch: Submarine Cables.
Depot Maintenance & Cable Stocks
57 Power Branch: Officer-in-Charge
58 Submarine Branch: Officer-in-Charge.
Laying & Maintenance Operations
42 Telegraph Branch: Officer-in-Charge
43 Deputy
44 Subs. Apparatus & Misc. Branch Telephone
Exchange Systems & Trunk Switching:
Officer-in-Charge
45 Subscribers' Apparatus & Miscellaneous
& Telephone Exchange Systems & Trunk
Switching Group
45 Telegraph Branch: General Questions
45 Provision of Telegraph Circuits & Equipment for:
Air Ministry, Admiralty, Foreign Office, GCHQ,
War Office & Other Users
63-65 Additional Suite

INLAND TELECOMMUNICATIONS
20 Principal
25 Assistant Secretary
27 Director
39 Circuit Utilisation Control: Officer-in-Charge
40 Telephone Operating & Routing: Officer-in-Charge
41 Telephone Operating & Routing
41A Circuit Utilisation Control
46 Priorities
47 Equipment Plans
48 Telegraph Service: Plans
59 Provision of Service: Officer-in-Charge
59A Telephone Service: Liaison Duty
60 Provision of Service: General Questions, Air Ministry,
Ministry of Aviation
61 Provision of Service: Admiralty, Foreign Office, GCHQ,
GCB, MOD, Home Office, War Office, UKLF

GENERAL DIRECTORATE
23 Liaison Officer
24 Private Secretary
26 Director-General

Above: The fourteen-position manual international switchboard in the underground telephone exchange, viewed from the supervisor's desk.

Above: The forty-position GPO sleeve-control auto-manual trunk switchboard on the left-hand side, facing the international switchboard on the right. According to a British Telecom survey made in the 1982, at least some of this equipment was manufactured in the 1940s, suggesting that it was transferred from the earlier exchange complex in Area 1.

Above: The international switchboard, viewed from the west end with the directory enquiries desk visible in the background. Although outwardly similar to the inland trunk switchboard opposite, the internal arrangement of this unit is distinctively different in order to cope with the various switching and signalling protocols that its connection will encounter abroad.

Above: Shortly after the CGWHQ was declassified in 2004 selected members of the press were invited to tour the site. For the benefit of the visiting journalists, maintenance staff brought many items out of store in order to create an image of what the headquarters might have looked like under operational conditions. Amongst the items on display in the manual exchange area are a number of telephone operators' chairs, still in their original 1960s protective wrapping, and a rack of operators' headsets.

Above left: The two-position directory enquiries desk. The grey shelving unit to the left of this photograph contained a complete collection of *Yellow Pages* for 1988, the last year for which updates were provided in the CGWHQ exchange.

Above right: Detailed view of a single position on the sleeve-control auto-manual trunk exchange, unusual in that it is not provided with charge metering equipment.

Right: General view of the manual exchange with the inland trunk switchboard on the right, international switchboard in the left background, directory enquiry desk in the left middle-ground and the supervisor's desk in the foreground.

Opposite above: The design of the CGWHQ exchange followed GPO convention in that space was provided for future expansion. Evidence of this can, for example, be seen in the numbering of the manual exchange positions; the inland positions are numbered 1-40, the international positions 101-114. Space was allocated to the west of the manual switch-room for additional switchboard positions while the area in this photograph was available for extensions to the internal automatic exchange and the telegraph exchange.

Opposite below left: The GPO maintenance engineers' rest room.

Opposite below right: Telephone cables entering the exchange via an underground duct in the Main Distribution Frame (MDF) room.

Above: Relay racks in the internal automatic exchange. Note the distinctive black and white tiles in this area.

Opposite: Uniselector racks in the internal automatic exchange. There was provision for 1,500 internal extension telephones, 1,394 of which were allocated, each of which was wired back to its own uniselector on this rack in order to offer the greatest operational flexibility. Space was available on the frame for a further 500 uniselectors should the need arise.

Right: Distribution frame and fuse racks in the automatic exchange.

Below left: The CGWHQ exchange included a trunk repeater and transmission station. The rack in the foreground contains supervisory equipment including a ringer bay, tone generators and alarm relays.

Below right: Another view of the repeater station showing the maintenance engineer's desk, an engineer's auxiliary test rack in the centre background and racks of repeater amplifiers in the left background.

Opposite: Channel oscillator racks and auxiliary test rack in the automatic telegraph exchange. Note the bottom indicator of the column of fault lamps partially obscured by black and yellow tape wrapped around the ladder on the left of this view. When illuminated it would indicate a fault with telegraph transmission equipment in Area 21, the government communications centre.

Above: A thinly populated section of the distribution frame in the transmission station. The identification letters indicate it is a part of a very extensive frame.

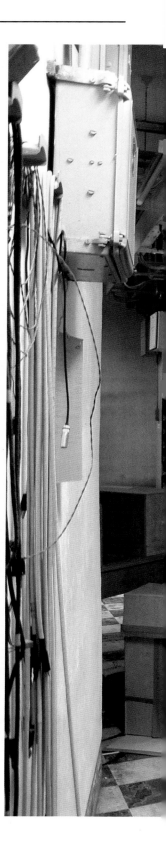

Above: A mobile test unit in the transmission section. The unit to the left of the passageway appears to be a rectifier cabinet.

Right: Channel carrier equipment racks in the transmission area, with repeater racks in the background.

Above: Motor generator in the telephone exchange power room. This machine and its associated equipment converted 415V three-phase from the mains or from the standby generator plant into a smooth DC current to run the telephone apparatus and charge the station batteries.

Right: High voltage distribution and monitoring panel in the power room. One of a group of three Brentford AC regulators can be seen in the right background.

Left: A group of rectifiers in the exchange power room.

Left: Engineer's test switchboard, with a pair of test jack panels to the right, in the Main Distribution Frame room.

Below left: Although there were 1,394 designated telephone positions under the original SUBTERFUGE scheme, no handsets were ever put in place either then or under the later reduced-area schemes. Instead, the telephones were kept in the GPO store-room ready for distribution when the headquarters was activated.

Below right: A section of the central battery room. Originally this room would have been filled with glass-cased, lead-acid accumulators mounted on rows of wooden racks similar to that seen on the right-hand side of this photograph. They were removed after the exchange was closed as a health and safety precaution. Note the acid-proof quarry-tiled floor.

Above: The Lister Blackstone standby generator plant in the GPO emergency generating station.

Right: The power distribution and monitoring panel in the GPO emergency generating station.

Left: A selection of GPO ladders stored in the emergency generating station. The ladder labelled 'Auto' originated in the automatic telegraph exchange. The Lister Blackstone generator set and its associated switchgear is visible in the background.

NORTH AIR DRIFT

P43

SUB STATION

HOSPITAL

FEMALE WC

MALE WC

KEY TO AREA 9

STORES

DORMITORIES

FEMALE WCS

MALE WCS

PLANT

Area 9 was the central stores and carried a vast array of equipment and consumables required for the day-to-day running of the CGWHQ. The stockholding included catering equipment, janitorial supplies, huge volumes of paper, envelopes, paperclips, rubber bands, red-tape and all the other stationery paraphernalia associated with the administration of government. Prior to 1970 the stores contained, amongst a myriad other items, more than 11,000,000 sheets of copy paper, 100,000 rubber bands, 10,000 ballpoint pens, 250 sticks of sealing wax and 400 typewriters. By 1975, under the reduced-area scheme, these quantities were somewhat scaled down, but the stores still held some 3,000,000 sheets of copy paper and more than a million sheets of typing paper in various sizes. The number of typewriters was, however, reduced to just forty, which appears a very meagre number with which to rule a nation. Furniture stocks included 250 bedsteads, 1,925 two-tier bunks, 4,600 mattresses, 9,086 folding chairs and almost 1,000 tubular steel stacking chairs, along with 2,320 folding wooden tables, 4,260 lockers and 350 filing cabinets.

Above: A corner of the stores area with, in the foreground, a number of tubular steel chairs, manufactured in 1961 and still in their original paper wrapping. On top of them there are a number of steel waste paper bins, also in their original packaging. The steel drums in the background contain silica gel, a desiccant used to absorb atmospheric moisture.

Left: General view of the stationery storage racks in Area 9. The pillar immediately behind the pile of pallets in the middle distance is numbered P43. Using this pillar number as a guide, it is possible to identify the location from which this photograph was taken on the plan reproduced on page 109.

Above: A process camera, for the use of one of the reprographic units located in the CGWHQ.

Left: A variety of different types of typing paper and telex rolls in the stationery store. Each box carries a code identifying its owning department and the location of its end-user. The numbers in the 1200-1299 series contained within a red triangle denote that they are for the use of the War Cabinet. The designation R2/21 denote that it is destined for room 2 in Area 21, the typing and duplicating room in the government communications centre.

Above, below and left: An esoteric collection of catering utensils and equipment, all of which have remained unused since the early 1960s.

Above left: Amongst the more unusual things in the catering section of the stores was this green-painted DDT insecticide sprayer.

Above: Kettles, colanders, buckets, flour bins, mixing bowls and milk jugs. Just a few of the necessities for an industrial-scale catering facility.

Below left: A few of the 250 salt dispensers in the catering store (one for each of the 225 canteen tables plus a few extra to replace breakages).

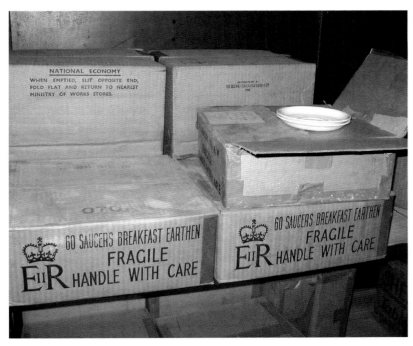

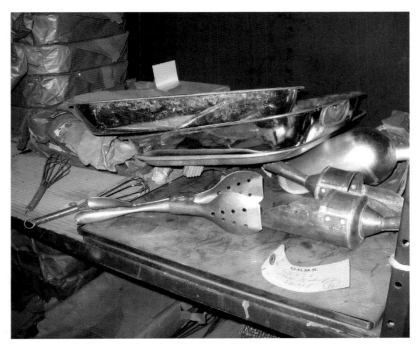

Above: Part of the stockpile of 2,320 breakfast saucers. There was a similar number of standard saucers along with the cups to complement them.
Below: Kitchen knives and meat cleavers. The stores also contained 2,320 dessert spoons and 1,160 each of fish knives, dinner knives and forks.

Above: Baking trays, flour scoops, hand whisks and a tea-bag squeezer; all fifty years old and unused.
Below: Perhaps something of an extravagance given the circumstances: this is a 'Butapatta' butter pat machine.

Above: Secure cabinets and safes awaiting dispersal to the rooms to which they have been allocated.

Right: A few of the 2,000 grey steel waste paper bins provided for the CGWHQ, nearly all of which remain in store in the manufacturer's wrapping.

Left: Janitorial supplies, including detergents (28 gallons in plastic containers), disinfectants, scouring powder, sweeping brushes, toilet brushes, broom handles and drain cleaners. The large paper-covered cylinders between the racks in the middle distance are rolls of linoleum.

Above: Each government department was asked to provide a list of reference books that they would require. Amongst those requested by the Foreign & Commonwealth Office was *A Guide to Diplomatic Practice*. One could think, perhaps, that it was a little late to learn the arts of diplomacy.

Opposite: Stapling machines and balls of string: essential requirements for national survival in a post holocaust world.

THE HOSPITAL

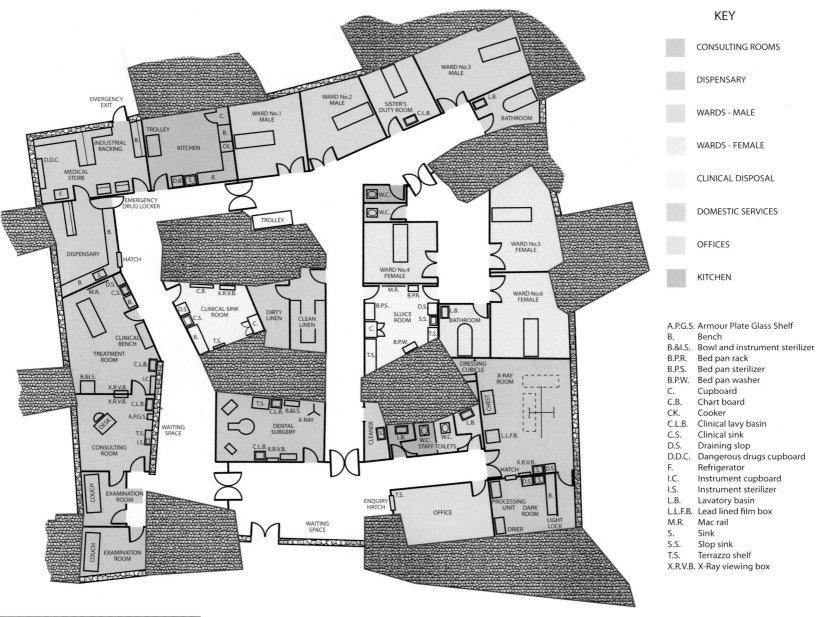

KEY

- CONSULTING ROOMS
- DISPENSARY
- WARDS - MALE
- WARDS - FEMALE
- CLINICAL DISPOSAL
- DOMESTIC SERVICES
- OFFICES
- KITCHEN

A.P.G.S.	Armour Plate Glass Shelf
B.	Bench
B.&I.S.	Bowl and instrument sterilizer
B.P.R.	Bed pan rack
B.P.S.	Bed pan sterilizer
B.P.W.	Bed pan washer
C.	Cupboard
C.B.	Chart board
CK.	Cooker
C.L.B.	Clinical lavy basin
C.S.	Clinical sink
D.S.	Draining slop
D.D.C.	Dangerous drugs cupboard
F.	Refrigerator
I.C.	Instrument cupboard
I.S.	Instrument sterilizer
L.B.	Lavatory basin
L.L.F.B.	Lead lined film box
M.R.	Mac rail
S.	Sink
S.S.	Slop sink
T.S.	Terrazzo shelf
X.R.V.B.	X-Ray viewing box

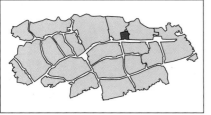

The CGWHQ hospital lies to the southeast of the stores and is accessible from East Main Road. It was originally intended that the hospital should be much larger and include forty single-bed wards and an operating theatre. The cost of this, however, was deemed prohibitive, particularly as such a scheme would have required a dedicated ventilation system to avoid the transmission of contagious diseases through the central air-conditioning plant. The hospital would deal with only day-to-day ailments; more serious cases would be transferred to conventional hospitals, should any have survived.

Above: The hospital reception area. The first door on the left is the dentist's surgery, the double-doors give on to a corridor leading to the wards, the next two doors are to the staff toilets and the room at the end of the short corridor is the x-ray department.

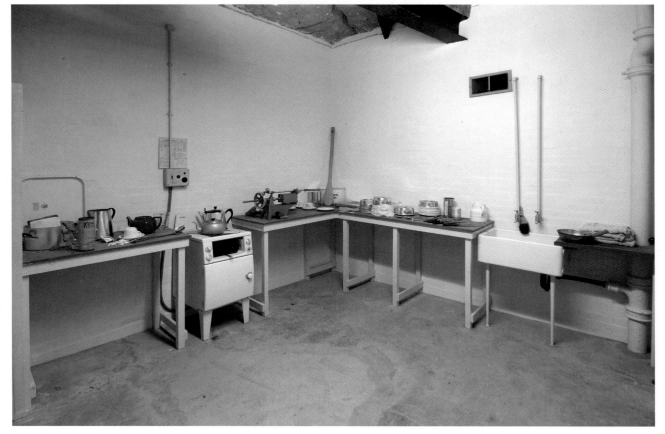

Above left: The closed door on the right is the Duty Nurse's office, the double-doors at the end of the corridor lead to the kitchen, dispensary and treatment room, the double-doors in the left foreground lead to the female patients' wards.

Above right: The doors to the left give access to the female wards, the room at the end of the corridor is the female patients' bathroom.

Left: The hospital kitchen, somewhat over-equipped (with, amongst other things, a rather misplaced sanitary towel bin) by maintenance staff for the benefit of visiting journalists.

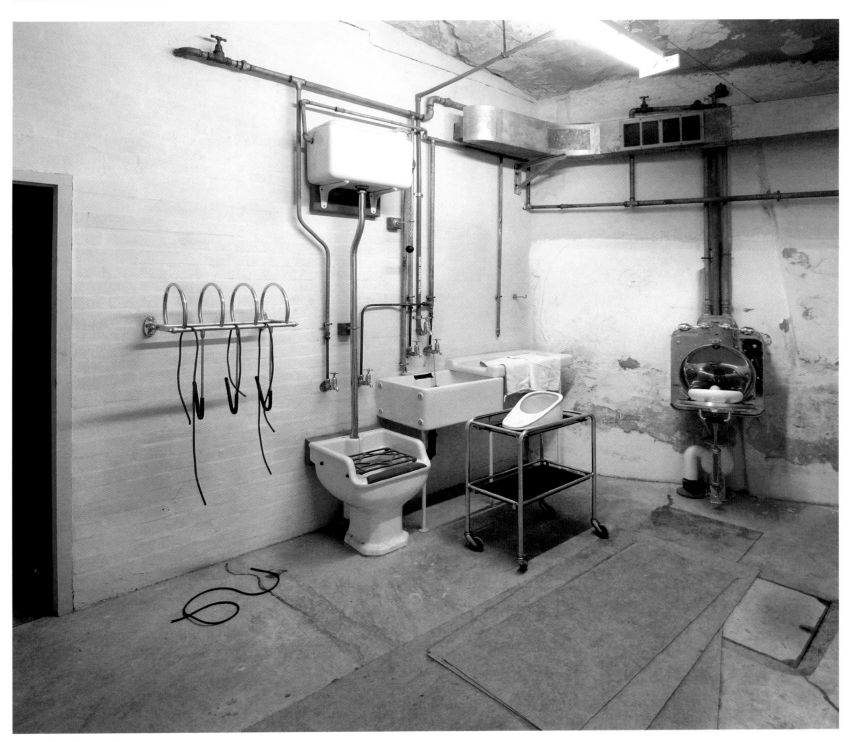

Above: The clinical sluice room.

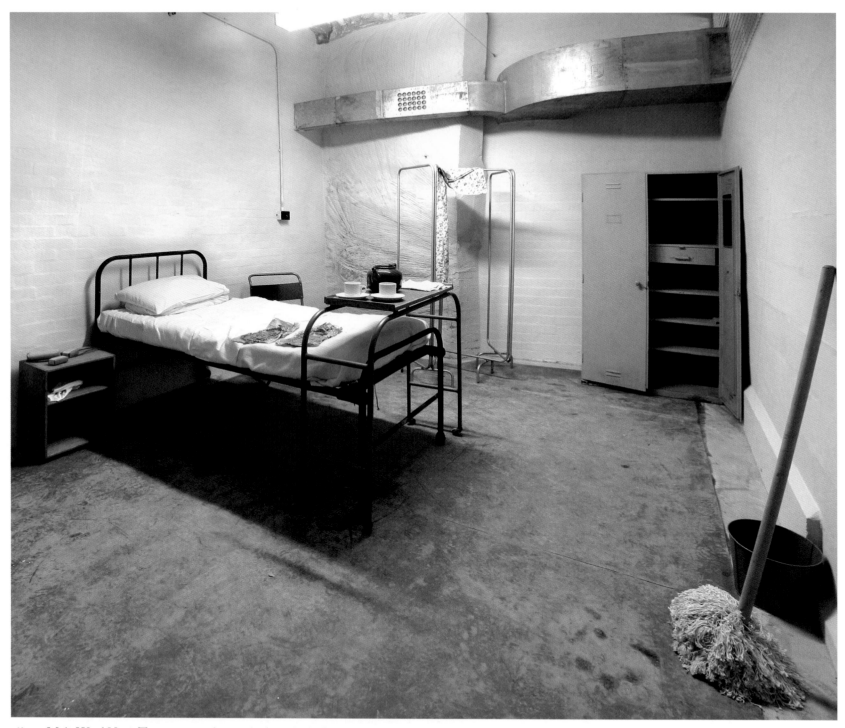

Above: Male Ward No.1. The strange red items laid on the bed are rubber hot water bottles in sealed bags.

Above: Male Ward No.2.

Below: The Duty Nurse's office, on the male wards corridor.

Above: The dark-room in the x-ray processing unit. This was separated from the main x-ray room by a light-lock. All the x-ray equipment was removed and transferred to the Bristol Royal Infirmary in the late 1970s.

Below: Interior view of the dispensary showing the service hatch.

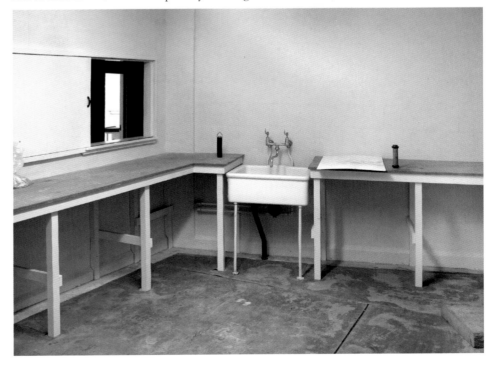

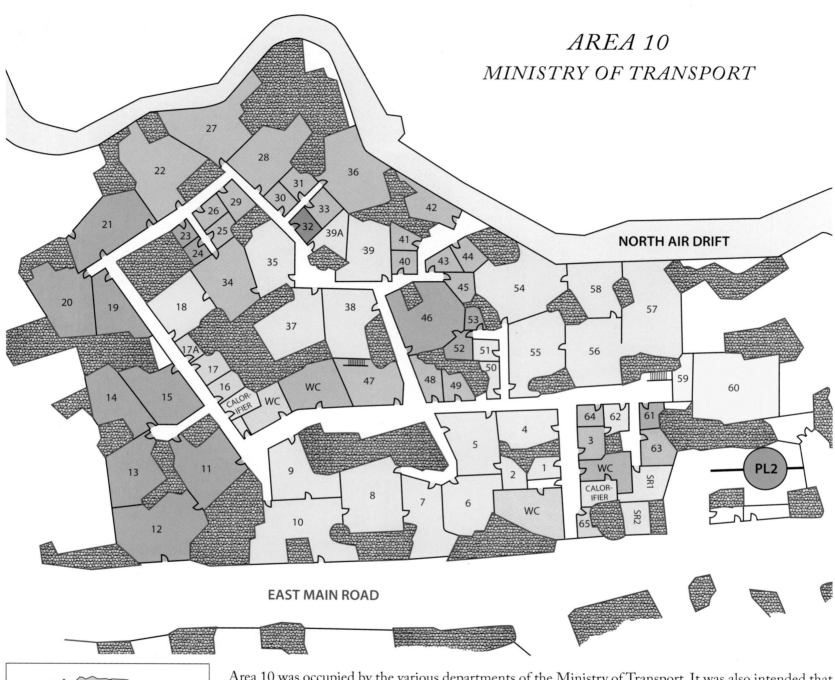

AREA 10
MINISTRY OF TRANSPORT

27

22

28

36

31

30

29

26

33

21

23

25

32

39A

24

35

39

41

42

34

40

43

44

NORTH AIR DRIFT

20

19

18

38

45

54

58

37

46

53

57

17A

52

51

55

56

17

50

16

WC

47

48

49

59

60

CALOR-
IFIER

WC

WC

14

15

64

62

61

4

3

63

PL2

5

13

11

9

WC

SR1

2

1

CALOR-
IFIER

8

7

6

SR2

65

WC

10

12

EAST MAIN ROAD

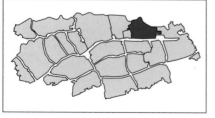

Area 10 was occupied by the various departments of the Ministry of Transport. It was also intended that the NATO civil agencies should be co-located here but, as we have seen earlier in this book, this was a controversial proposal that was never fully resolved. It is evident from the office allocations that the greater emphasis was put upon shipping and overseas supplies, particularly the acquisition of food and oil, rather than inland distribution, by road, rail and canal, the oversight of which was administered from just three rooms.

KEY TO AREA 10

SHIPPING OPERATIONS
1   Head of Convoy
4   Convoy Staff
8   Bunkering
9,10 Tankers (Allocation & Operation)
50 Principal Shipping Controller, Typist
51 Controller of Sea Transport
54 Sea Transport Staff
56 Troops
57 Liners, Coasting & Short Sea
58 Sea Transport Staff
Shipping Services
2   Controller of Port Services
5   Port Service Staff
6   Loading
7   Repairs & Crew
8   Stores
18 Shipping & Intelligence Staff
35,37-38 Shipping & Intelligence Staff
39 Statistics Staff
39A Director of Shipping Intelligence
55 Port Service Staff
62 Shipping & Planning Staff

PRINCIPALS
3   Private Secretary, Typist
48 Deputy Secretary (Shipping), Typist
49 Under-Secretary (Policy & Planning), Typist
63 Minister
64 Permanent Secretary

SHIPPING POLICY & PLANNING
11,12 Civil Requirements (Dry Cargo)
13 Requisitioning of Ships
14,15,19-21 Tonnage Planning & Ship Allocation (Dry Cargo)

ESTABLISHMENT
16 Establishment Liaison Officer
17 Establishment Staff
65 Messenger

COMMONWEALTH & ALLIED SHIPPING REPRESENTATIVES
22 Commonwealth & Allied Shipping Representatives
25,26 Allied Shipping Representatives
27 Allied Shipping Representatives (Coastal Group)
29-31,33,34,40-45 Allied Shipping Representatives

NATO AGENCY LIAISON
23,24 NATO Agency Liaison

DSEB SECRETARIAT
28 DSEB Secretariat
36 DSEB Board Room

DJEB COMMITTEE ROOM
32 DJEB Committee Room

INLAND TRANSPORT
46 Road Transport Under-Secretary,
    Railway Control Staff, Road Transport Staff
52 Deputy Secretary
53 Railway Control Officer
61 Typing Staff

SIGNALS
47 Signals Section

MAP ROOM
59 Viewing Room
60 Map Room

Above: A narrow access passageway between offices in the Ministry of Transport area. This is typical of the rather claustrophobic corridors throughout the CGWHQ.

Above: One of the headquarters' eleven mobile tea trolleys, parked in a passageway in Area 10.

Left: A typical office in Area 10 laid out as a Type 'A' room, which would serve as a combined working and sleeping area. The arrangement seen here verges towards the luxurious; the original specification allowed only one folding wooden table, two un-upholstered folding wooden chairs and one tubular steel chair. There should also be a steel wardrobe and a two-drawer filing cabinet.

Above: Area 10 room 60, the Ministry of Transport conference and map room. This room is overlooked by an enclosed, high-level glazed balcony (room 59). This arrangement of map room and high-level glazed mezzanine can be found in several other areas including the Cabinet Office section of Area 14 (rooms 44 and 45) and the UKLF section of area 18 (rooms 2 and 3). The black pipe at ceiling level carries seepage water from shaft E1A to a sump in the east lung. From there the waste water is pumped into a culvert that runs beneath Box Tunnel.

AREA 11
PLANT ROOMS & WORKSHOPS

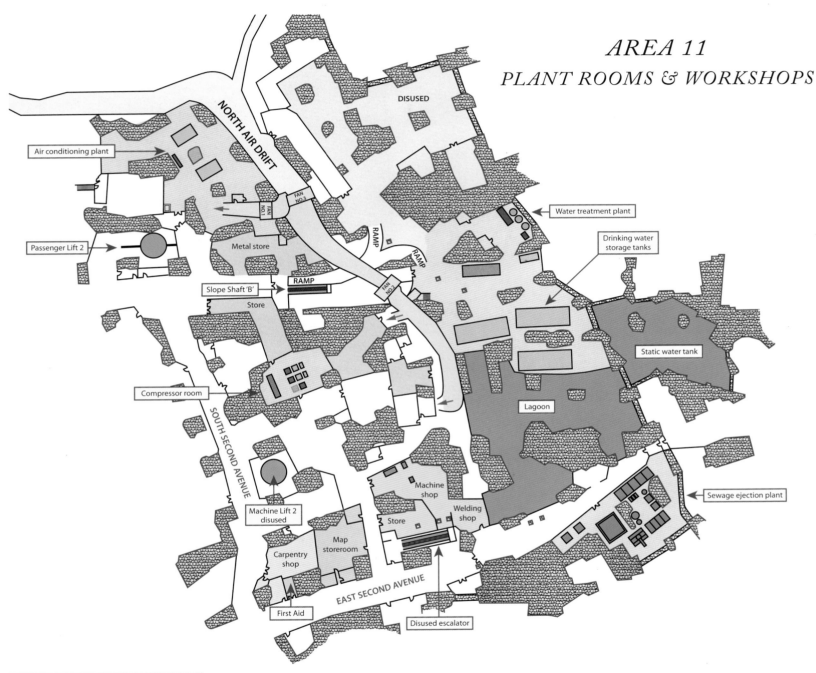

Air conditioning plant

NORTH AIR DRIFT

DISUSED

FAN NO.1

FAN NO.3

Passenger Lift 2

Metal store

RAMP

RAMP

FAN NO.2

Water treatment plant

Drinking water storage tanks

Slope Shaft 'B'

Store

Static water tank

Compressor room

SOUTH SECOND AVENUE

Lagoon

Machine Lift 2 disused

Machine shop

Welding shop

Sewage ejection plant

Store

Map storeroom

Carpentry shop

EAST SECOND AVENUE

First Aid

Disused escalator

Area 11 was the domain of the Ministry of Works & Building (later DoE and PSA) maintenance department, and housed the CGWHQ water supply and storage facilities, sewage treatment works and the east end air-conditioning and ventilation plant. Facilities here include well-equipped woodwork, mechanical engineering and welding shops and raw materials stores. Two underground reservoirs, one internal and one outside the secure perimeter of the headquarters (the latter added in 1982) provided cooling water for the generating station and a reserve of untreated water for domestic use.

Left: Pipework and control equipment at the rear of the Sulzer units. The red pipes in the foreground carry condenser water to radiators in the adjacent fan chamber; the asbestos-lagged pipeline in the background, near the wall behind a pair of auxiliary heat exchangers, carry chilled water to the associated dehumidifier units.

Right: Hot and chilled water pipelines entering the north air drift. At this point, banks of electrostatic filter in the airways remove contamination from incoming air. The adjustable louvres help control the mix of fresh and recirculated air flowing through the headquarters, depending upon the ambient humidity.

Opposite: The east plant room with Sulzer refrigeration units Nos. 3 and 4. After the area reduction of 1968 the west plant was shut down and these two units took over the air-conditioning load of the rest of the surviving areas of the headquarters. Their approaching obsolescence and increasing unreliability were factors in the decision to dispense with the CGWHQ in the early years of the twenty-first century.

Above left: The pronounced hump in the floor marks the point where a major airway descends into the under-floor ducts. At the right-hand end the airway connected to the plenum chamber of one of the large circulating fans installed during the Second World War.

Above: When the ventilation system was modified to serve the CGWHQ the old fans were replaced by smaller, more efficient units similar to these.

Left: Under the modified CGWHQ ventilation scheme all the ventilation shafts giving direct access to the protected area were sealed off in order to prevent the ingress of contaminated outside air. Instead, air was drawn from the disused quarry workings to the east and west of the central area, known respectively as the east and west lungs. Outside air entered the lungs some distance from the CGWHQ perimeter and, in the humid days of summer, deposited much of its water vapour in the relatively cold quarry which acted as a heat-sink and thus reduced the load on the air-conditioning plants. Air was drawn into the CGWHQ via venturi tubes in the perimeter wall, a group of which can be seen in this photograph. The action that would be taken in the event of a nuclear attack was somewhat primitive: Two men would be despatched to each lung with instructions to bolt-down pre-positioned steel plates over the orifices after having inserted wooden bungs into them.

Above left: The partially demolished surface superstructure of ventilation shaft E1A, known colloquially as the 'Queen Mary' shaft on account of its very large size. Following the closure of the CGWHQ the shaft-top structure was demolished and the area subsequently built over.

Middle left: A vertiginous view down into the top of the 100-foot-deep vertical shaft.

Below left: This view of the inlet side of the surface fan-chamber for the Queen Mary shaft gives some idea of its scale. The fifteen-foot diameter fan was mounted across the two horizontal concrete ledges seen in the foreground.

Above: The base of E1A shaft in the north air drift. Because the CGWHQ ventilation system was largely recirculatory with only relatively small volumes of air exhausted to the atmosphere, E1A was rendered redundant. The bottom of the shaft was plugged with concrete with just a couple of small exhaust ducts passing through it.

Above: The drained lagoon or underground water reservoir. This, together with a second static water tank constructed outside the CGWHQ perimeter provided a reserve of cooling water for the engines in the emergency generating plant and, if necessary, domestic purposes.

Within Area 11 there existed a complex network of three interlinked water systems: domestic treatment and supply, engineering services supply, and waste water disposal. Under normal circumstances domestic water would be taken from reservoirs on the surface, but if for any reason these were lost then it was possible to fall back upon the reserves stored in the lagoons,

which was normally used for engine cooling. This, however, could be rendered potable via a chlorine dosing plant. Treated water was stored in three large steel tanks with a total capacity of 100,000 gallons. The lagoon could, in emergency, be topped up from the copious amounts of spring water arising underground within the quarry. A complex system of pump-houses and sumps was established in the east lung to control the excess spring water, which was pumped into a drainage culvert beneath Box railway tunnel and ultimately into Box Brook. Seepage water from the various air shafts and inclines was dealt with in a similar manner.

Above: Chlorine dosing tanks in the water treatment plant.

Left: Raw water storage tank adjacent to the treatment plant.

Above: The complexity of the drinking water supply system can be gauged from the intricate maze of pipework in this photograph. In the foreground is a group of transfer pumps. Two of the pipelines are labelled 'potable water' and 'treated drinking water' respectively. The large red pipe at roof level appears to be carrying cooling water from the power station. The upright cylinder with an open manhole to the right is a pressure cylinder for the drinking water supply cistern. Visible in the background are two of the main water storage tanks.

Left: Exterior view of one of the pump-houses located in the east lung that control the flow of water from the underground springs that give Spring Quarry its name. Beyond the pump-house, surrounded by a red steel safety rail is a storm water suction chamber. Under stable conditions, spring water and drainage water from the CGWHQ flows by gravitation, via a 215mm pipe, through the storm water chamber and into a culvert below Box Tunnel. Under abnormal weather conditions the excess water is pumped via this pump-house up a delivery pipe in a borehole to the surface.

Below left: One of a pair of centrifugal pumps used to pump storm water to the surface.

Below right: Switchgear for controlling the storm water pumps. The numbering of the pumps, and the range of alternative electricity supplies available to power them, gives some indication of how important the prevention of flooding was to safety of the CGWHQ.

Above: Vertical compressors providing air for the pneumatic ejectors in the sewage treatment plant. Initially the CGWHQ made use of the existing factory sewage disposal system, constructed in 1941, with little alteration. Later, however, a more modern sewage ejection system was installed to replace it and the wartime plant subsequently fell into disuse. Using the wartime system raw sewage could be pumped to the surface but, if the surface system was disabled, the treatment plant had the capacity to neutralise effluent and dispose of it in remote areas underground.

Left: General view of the sewage treatment works looking across the sludge tanks with the primary collection tanks (brick-built, with a red steel railing on top) in the background. When this photograph was taken the plant had been long disused; three electric effluent pumps connected to the array of black pipework in the background have been removed along with the sludge pumps that would have been mounted on the white concrete bases in the middle of the image behind the sludge tank railings. The tall concrete structure to the left is a coagulating tank.

Left: A view from the top of the primary collection tanks towards the sludge tanks. The green steel tanks to the left are caustic soda vessels. One of the functions of caustic soda in the treatment of sewage was to inhibit the production of hydrogen sulphide and thus help deodorise the final effluent.

Right: Air receivers, manufactured during the Second World War for service in the Bristol Aeroplane Company's underground factory, still in use providing compressed air for general works services in the CGWHQ and to operate the new sewage ejection system.

Below left: Two of the three radial compressors in the central compressor room. These, like the air receivers, are of Second World War vintage. A third unit, to the right of those visible in this photograph, is partially dismantled and has been out of use for many years.

Below right: Pressure switches and automatic control gear for the compressors. Like the compressors and air receivers, these pieces of equipment carry small engraved plates recording their wartime origins with the Ministry of Aircraft Production.

Above: A general view of the engineers' maintenance workshop. This well-equipped facility included a reasonably modern Colchester Student 1800 lathe and a 1960s Wicksteed electric hacksaw. Some of the machines, including the Asquith vertical drill, the Denbigh grinder and Wolf pedestal grinder seen in this photograph appear much older and were probably inherited from the wartime factory.

Above: The carpentry shop was particularly well equipped and has the appearance of a small manufacturing facility rather than a maintenance workshop. In this picture can be seen one of the two large Dominion combined saw-benches and thicknesser/planers provided in the workshop. There is also a smaller, more modern Wadkin saw-bench in the room through the arch in the centre background.

Above left: The second saw-bench and thicknesser/planer in the woodwork shop, together with a large, floor-mounted bandsaw in the background.

Above right: This morticing machine in the woodwork shop appears to be of pre-war design and may be another piece of equipment inherited from the Bristol Aeroplane Company.

Left: The welding shop. The device mounted on the bench in the centre of the photograph is a hand-operated sheet-metal guillotine.

Above, below left and below right: Maintenance work in the CGWHQ involved much moving of heavy machinery. Here we see some of the chain hoists, hydraulic jacks, D-rings, strops and chains required to facilitate this.

Above: A small, hand-operated 7-cwt mobile crane. The two vertical pumps in the background pump waste water and sludge from the laundry and kitchen to the surface for disposal.

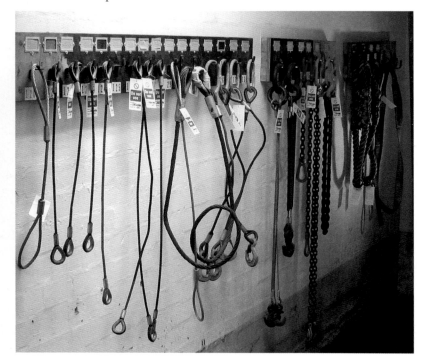

Above: Part of the varied fleet of electric trucks available for the use of maintenance staff, parked in the battery charging bay. Vehicles seen here include fork-lift trucks, flat-bed goods wagons and personnel transporters. The red vehicle near the rear wall is a street-cleaning machine.

Right: General view of the maintenance staff domestic and office accommodation. In recent years many of the reference books previously held in the Area 9 stores have been moved to this room in an ineffectual attempt to protect them from damp. We have seen already that the Foreign & Commonwealth Office requested a copy of Sir Ernest Satow's *A Guide to Diplomatic Practice*; titles requested by other departments included *Kessing's Contemporary Archives*, Callaham's *Russian-English Technical and Chemical Dictionary*, *The Times Guide to the House of Commons* (why?), *Pacific Islands Pilot*, *Cassell's Encyclopaedia of Literature*, *Lloyd's Register*, *The Statutes Revised*, *The Medical Directory*, *Times Atlas* and *Whitaker's Almanac*.

Below left: Plan chests containing engineering drawings of plant and equipment on site.

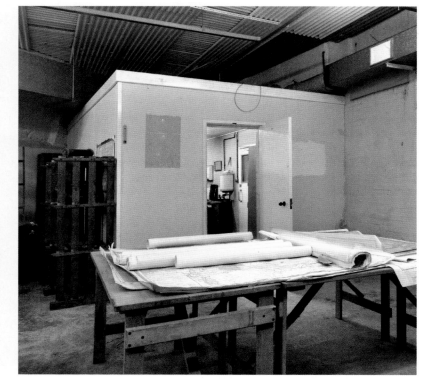

Above: The maintenance engineers' 90-day store, containing all the spares, consumables, tools and equipment required to ensure the smooth running of the headquarters during the three months immediately following attack, during which time it was assumed that external re-supply would be impossible. Although part of the site maintenance facility, these stores are actually located in the southeast corner of the catering complex in Area 12, occupying the former dining area of the south servery that became redundant when the headquarters was reduced in scale in the late 1960s.

Opposite below right: Maintenance staff would be expected to work and sleep in this area under operational conditions. The accommodation provided included a small kitchen, seen here. To the left of the kitchen is a wooden rack containing spare Lamson canisters.

Layout of Area 12
1959 - 1968

KEY TO AREA 12

- DINING AREA
- KITCHEN
- SERVERIES
- LAUNDRY
- FEMALE WC
- MALE WC
- SHOWERS
- PLANT
- STORES

In its original configuration, Area 12 accommodated the eastern kitchen and restaurant, which provided twenty-four hour sustenance for the predominantly senior staff working in the War Cabinet area and associated key departments nearby. Originally the centrally positioned kitchen was surrounded by dining areas and had three separate serveries from which diners could collect their meals. Hot beverages could be obtained from an island coffee-bar in the west dining room.

*Layout of Area 12
1969 - 2004*

KEY TO AREA 12

- DINING AREA
- KITCHEN
- SERVERIES
- LAUNDRY
- FEMALE WC
- MALE WC
- SHOWERS
- PLANT
- STORES

After the 1968 reorganisation the southern and eastern dining rooms were abandoned and their serveries dismantled, the south dining room becoming an additional storage area for maintenance materials while the east dining room was reconfigured as a smaller scale laundry using equipment transferred from the original industrial laundry in Area 20. In more recent years part of the west dining room adjoining the furniture store has been used as an overflow depository for damp-affected paper previously held in Area 9.

Above: The west approach to the main servery in the central canteen. The dining areas associated with this servery are on a higher level and are connected by two separate railed inclines to the east and west of pillar No. T12. This arrangement facilitated the most efficient through-flow of customers at the counters. The great ceiling height in this area is due to the fact that during the factory era the quarry floor was chased out to give a minimum clearance of fifteen feet to accommodate very tall vertical milling machines.

Right: The east approach to the central servery. The kitchen is located behind the curtain wall to the rear of the counters.

Left: A view of the main servery from behind the counter showing the electrically heated bain-maries and hot-cupboards.

Opposite and above: Two views of the principal food preparation area showing the cylindrical steam-heated boilers, electric hotplates and small electric ovens. Behind the row of three boilers can be seen the backs of three large steam ovens. All the steam appliances would have been rendered unusable following the closure of the Spring Quarry boilerhouse in the mid-1990s.

Left: Front view of the steam ovens.

Below left: Two electrically heated deep-fat fryers in the central kitchen. The half-height wall to the right of the fryers marks the position of the northern servery which was sealed off when the kitchen and dining areas were revised in the late 1960s.

Below right: A walk-in refrigerator and a group of smaller refrigerators in the food storage area.

Above and below right: Hobart industrial dishwashers in what had, until 1968, been the returned crockery areas of the north and east serveries.
Below: An automatic potato-peeler and, to its left, a waste disposal machine.

Above: The double-sided island coffee bar, seen here, stands in the middle of the dining area. Although constructed in the early 1960s it reflects a vaguely art deco design, complemented by the stylishly period Stott coffee machines.

Left: A diner's-eye view of the coffee bar, with tables laid out by the maintenance staff prior to the press visit in 2005. All the furniture would normally have been kept under dust sheets in a store-room in the southwest corner of the dining area and would have been brought out only after the headquarters had become active.

Below left: Internal view of the coffee bar.

Below right: Detail of one of the two Stott coffee machines.

Above: When the capacity of the CGWHQ was reduced from a workforce of 4,000 to approximately 1,000 in 1968, much less extensive catering facilities were required. Two of the three serveries were closed down and the opportunity taken to convert the east servery and dining area into a more compact laundry, using one each of the washing machines, spin dryers, tumble dryers, coppers and blanket presses from the now abandoned industrial laundry in Area 20.

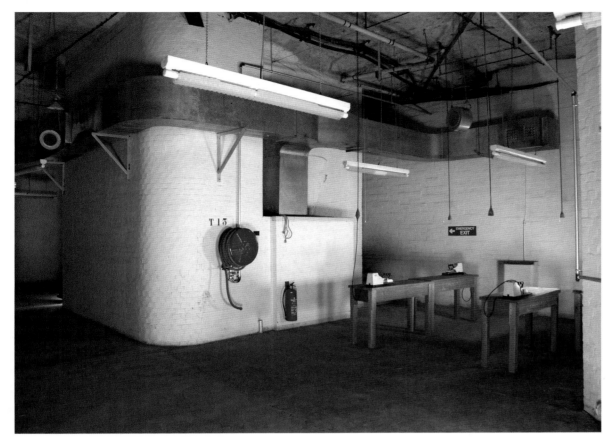

Left: Also recovered for re-use from the industrial laundry were the four ironing stations seen in this photograph.

Below left: Provision was also made for making minor repairs to bed linen and personal clothing using, amongst other things, both manual and electric Singer sewing machines.

Below right: Detail of an electric iron. The yellow label attached to the heat-resistant runners on this device was applied by Casella Hasmat Ltd and reads 'sample taken for analysis', following an asbestos hazard survey made in 2004. Asbestos, which is now regarded as highly carcinogenic, was widely used up until the late 1960s as a heat insulator. Its presence in Spring Quarry, particularly in the air-conditioning plants and as a pipeline insulator was one of the many factors that hastened the site's closure.

Above: To the north of the kitchen in Area 12 there is an extensive suite of ablutions. When the underground factory was constructed in the 1940s adequate toilet facilities were provided for a planned workforce of some 25,000 men and women. These survived virtually unchanged when the site was transformed into the CGWHQ, so, by 1970 when the working complement was reduced to little more than 1,000 the provision was extremely generous. The long trough-like sinks seen here in the gentlemen's ablutions are original wartime fixtures. Had the CGWHQ been activated, staff would have been expected to use these not just for personal hygiene but also to wash their clothes as the industrial laundry would have been used only for bed linen and catering cloths.

Right and below left: Gentlemen's toilets, with a hint of humour courtesy of the maintenance staff.

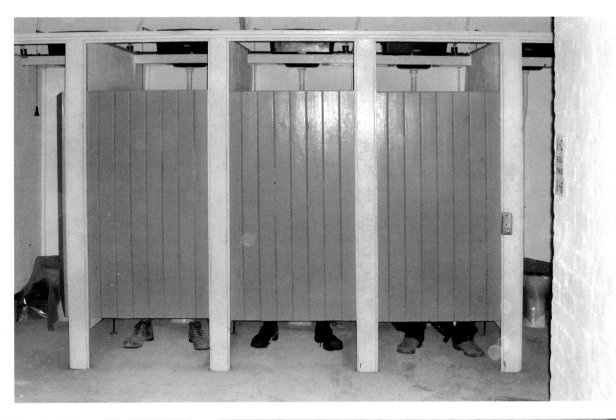

Below right: Showers in the gentlemen's wash-room. These, too, are original Second World War fixtures but their provision is much less generous.

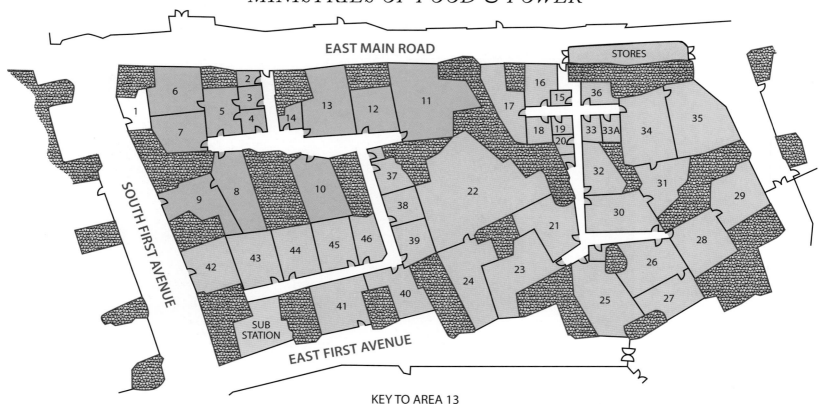

EAST MAIN ROAD

STORES

SOUTH FIRST AVENUE

SUB STATION

EAST FIRST AVENUE

KEY TO AREA 13

MINISTRY OF POWER
15 Messengers
16 Minister, Conference Room
17 Private Secretary to Minister, Chief of Staff,
   Private Secretary to Permanent Secretary,
   Clerical Officer Secretary
18 Permanent Secretary
20A Store
21 Clerical Officer
22 Clerical/Typing
25 Copy Typists
Gas & Electricity
19 Under-Secretary
21 Clerical Officer Secretary
32 Assistant to Under-Secretary, Electricity Industry Liaison,
   Gas Industry Liaison

Coal
20 Under-Secretary
21 Clerical Officer Secretary
29 Assistant to Under-Secretary, Coal Industry Liaison
Petroleum
23,24 Petroleum Executive, National & International
26,27 Commonwealth & Eastern Hemisphere Representatives
28 European other than NATO
30 Petroleum Executive, National & International
31 Petroleum Executive, National & International
33 Under-Secretary
33A Assistant to Under-Secretary
34 Supply, Bunkering & Coastal Movement
35 Internal Distribution
36 Deputy Secretary
37-46 European NATO including Military

MINISTRY OF AGRICULTURE, FISHERIES & FOOD
3 Minister
4 Permanent Secretary
5 Private Secretaries
6 Legal Advisor, Scientific Adviser,
  Assistant Scientific Adviser
7 Operations Room
8 Overseas Relations, Import Programmes
9 Secretariat
10 Agricultural Adviser, Under-Secretary (Agriculture),
   Assistant Secretary (Fisheries)
11 Clerical Section
12 Typing Pool
13 Port, Inland Transport, Warehousing,
   Commercial Advisers
14 Public Relations Officer, Office Controller

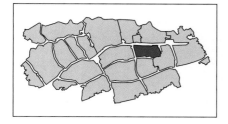

Under the SUBTERFUGE scheme, Area 13 was initially allocated to the Ministry of Power and Ministry of Agriculture, Fisheries & Food (MAFF). Very soon, however, Cabinet was told that due to the special nature of the MAFF role in wartime, there would be insufficient space at SUBTERFUGE to house the necessary staff. Alternative accommodation was earmarked at Aberystwyth University and in 1960 plans were prepared to utilise instead the nearby, and recently decommissioned, underground ammunition depot at Monkton Farleigh, under the code-name GULLY. Ultimately, neither plan was implemented.

Above: East Main Road, looking west from PL2. The double-doors visible in the middle distance give access to the Area 13 store-room. All the furniture for the MAFF offices, and all the bed frames, mattresses and linen for the dormitory would be stored here until the headquarters was called into action.

Below left and below right: Close-up views of the store-room. Upholstered chairs stored here are showing signs of serious mould damage. The large brown-paper packages behind the chairs are baled blankets which have similarly deteriorated in the damp environment.

AREA 14
WAR CABINET

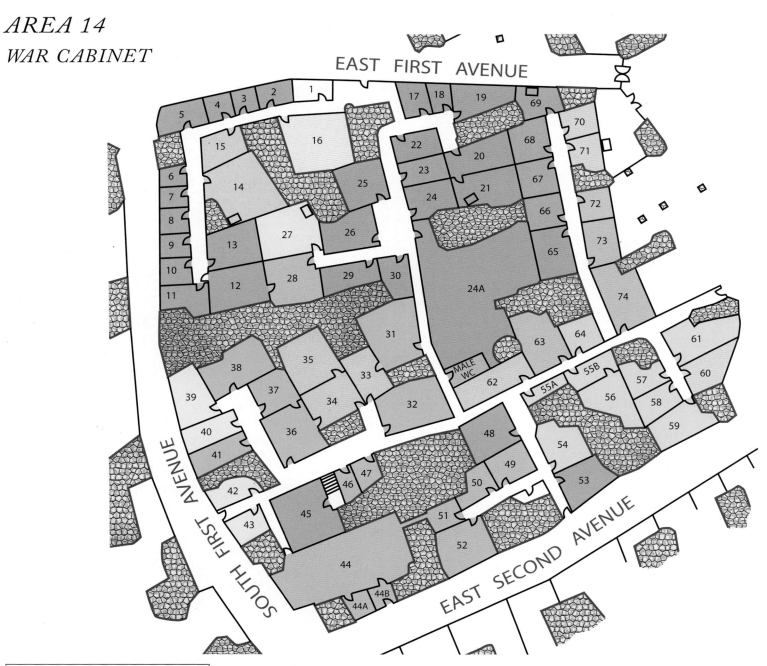

EAST FIRST AVENUE

SOUTH FIRST AVENUE

EAST SECOND AVENUE

MALE WC.

Located in Area 14, the War Cabinet, chaired by the Prime Minister (functioning also as Minister of Defence), together with the Home and Foreign Secretaries and three other senior ministers, would, in the constitutional terminology of the time, represent the 'ultimate source of authority'. In this role they would be supported by the Cabinet Secretariat and the Chiefs of the Defence staff and advised by the Joint Intelligence Committee. Key decisions made here would be disseminated via the Chiefs of Staff Committee, the Home Defence Committee and various overseas departments, depending upon context.

Above: The War Cabinet Map Room, overlooked by the viewing gallery of the Cabinet Office Conference Room on the right.

KEY TO AREA 14

WAR CABINET
2 Staff
3 War Cabinet Minister A
4 Staff
5 War Cabinet Minister B
6 War Cabinet Minister C
7 Staff
8 War Cabinet Minister D
9 Staff
10 War Cabinet Minister E
11 Staff
12 Ministerial Conference Room A
13 Ministerial Conference Room B
23 Ministerial Bedroom
45 Cabinet Office Conference Room, Waiting Room
48 Cabinet Office Conference Room, Waiting Room
53 Officer-in-Charge
66 Ministerial Bedroom
67 Ministerial Bedroom
68 Ministerial Bedroom
69 Ministerial Bedroom

TYPING POOL
14 Typing Pool
15 Officer-in-Charge

COMBINED REGISTRY COMMITTEE & DISTRIBUTION SECTIONS
16 Staff

MINISTRY OF DEFENCE
17 Director of LCSA
18 Deputy Director BJCEB
19 Co-Ordinator C-E Policy
20 BJCEB
21 Spare Room
22 Director of Forward Plans
24 Support Staff
25 BJCEB Support Staff
26 Chief Scientific Advisor
29 Under / Assistant Secretary
30 Deputy Secretary
65 MoD Sleeping Accommodation

MONITORS COMMUNICATORS / SECRETARIAT
28 Conference Room
63 Secretary, Staff
73 Foreign Office Monitors
74 GCHQ Communicators

CHIEF OF STAFF ORGANISATION
27 COS Conference Room
39 CDS Personal Staff
40 DCDS, ACDS
42 CDS
43 Staff Officer

PRIME MINISTER
31 Clerical Staff
33 Private Secretaries
34 Prime Minister
35 Prime Minister
62 Private Secretary's Bedroom

CABINET SECRETARIAT
Civil
32 Clerical Officers
36 Secretary to the Cabinet
37 Private Secretary
38 Civil Secretariat
46 Deputy, Under-Secretary
Military
31 Clerical Officers
38 GSO II
41 GSO I
47 Secretary, Deputy Secretary

MAP ROOM
44 Map Room
49 Staff
50 Officer-in-Charge
51 Staff
52 Draughtsmen and Clerical Staff

JOINT INTELLIGENCE COMMITTEE
54 JIC Director's Bedroom
55 Senior Mea Representative
56 JIC
57 Senior JIB Representative
58 Director GCHQ
59 Senior Service Representatives
61 Staff
64 JIC Sleeping Accommodation

JOINT PLANNING STAFF SECRETARIAT
60 Planning Staff
70 Deputy / Assistant Secretary
71 Clerical Staff

LIAISON
72 CIA / JIC Ottawa Representative

Door 44C allows access to the Map Room avoiding sensitive areas of the War Cabinet complex.

Above: Panorama of the Map Room.

Cabinet Office viewing gallery

FIRE EXIT

Door onto South First Avenue

Room 42 Chief of Defence Staff

Above: Main west-east passageway through the Cabinet Office.

Room 38 Cabinet Office Civil Secretariat

Narrow passageway communicating with offices of the Map Room staff.

Room 36
Cabinet Secretary

Room 32
Clerical Officers

Passage to offices of the Joint Intelligence Committee.

Above: Vestigial pieces of communications equipment left in the Foreign Office monitoring facility in room 73.

Left: The Cabinet Office Conference Room (room 24A), stacked full of furniture awaiting distribution to the various offices in Area 14. Had it been necessary to activate the CGWHQ then this room and the Cabinet Office Map Room would have become the nerve centre of the British government.

Right: The rooms on the right of this corridor are the Ministerial bedrooms (rooms 66-69). To the left are the offices of the Joint Planning Staff and various communications functions.

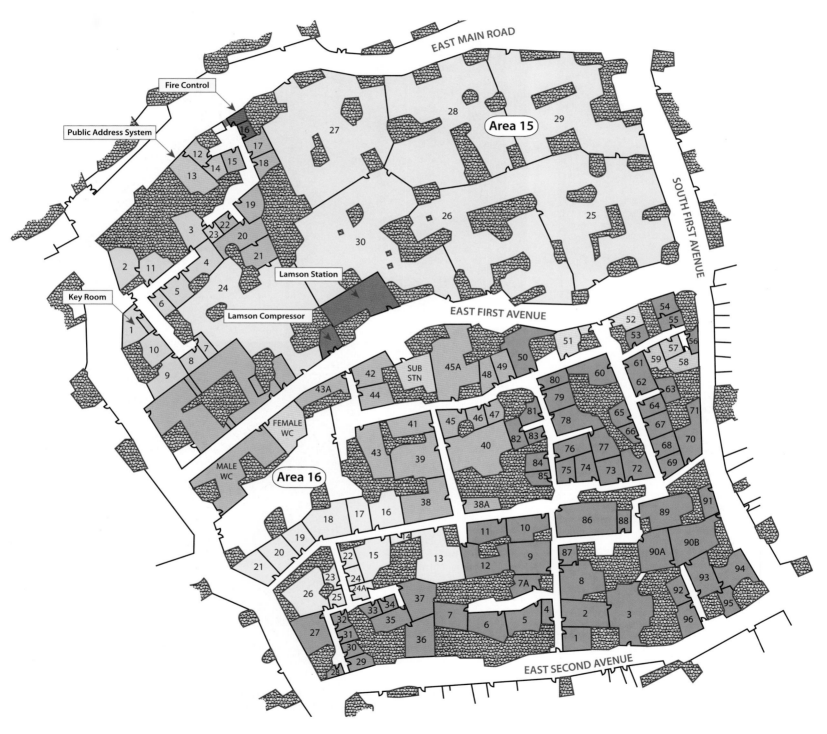

KEY TO AREA 15

ESTABLISHMENT OFFICERS BRANCH
1-2 Typing & Duplicating Pool
4 Personal Assistant, Clerical Section
5 Establishment Officer
6 Deputy Establishment Officer
7 Cashier, HEO (Office Services)
8 Welfare Officer
9 Chaplains
10 Chief Clerk, Controller of Office Services
11 Central Post Room
23 Stationery Section

PUBLIC ADDRESS SYSTEM
12 Battery Room
13 Control Room
14 Studio

CAMP COMMANDANT
15 Deputy Camp Commandant
16 Fire Control, Regimental Police
17 Information Room
18 Orderly Room
19 Administrative Officer, Guard Company Commander
20 Quartermaster
21 RSM
22 Camp Commandant

DORMITORIES
24-30

KEY TO AREA 16

HOME OFFICE
Home Defence Secretariat
1 Clerical Officer Secretaries
2 Assistant Secretary, Principals
3 Information Room 2
4 Chief Clerk, Executive Officer
5 Assistant Under-Secretary of State, Personal Assistant
6 GSO 1, Principals
7 Assistant Secretary, Brigadier
7A Clerical Officer Secretaries
9 Committee Room
86 Conference Room
88 Committee Clerks
89 Committee Room
90A Operations Room
90B Scientists' Room
91 Sorting & Despatch Clerks
92 Chief Scientific Adviser
93 Draughtsman/Photocopiers
94 Duplicating Room
Home Office
8 Communications Officers
53 Prison Commissioner, Personal Assistant

61 Police Duty Room
62 Staff
63 Assistant Under-Secretary of State
 Staff Officers
64 Principal, Assistant Principal
65 Assistant Prison Commissioner
66 Police Inspector
67 Clerical Officer Secretaries
68 Assistant Prison Commissioner
69 Assistant Under-Secretary of State
70 JI6
71 JI6
72 Assistant Under-Secretary of State, Personal Assistant
73 Deputy Under-Secretary of State
74 Assistant Secretary, Clerk
75 Assistant Secretary, Clerk
77 Legal Adviser, Clerk
78 Fire Staff (Control Room)
79 Fire Inspectors
80 Assistant Prison Commissioner, Clerk
82 Security Service
83 Security Service
84 SEO
85 Personal Assistant to Deputy Under-Secretary
87 SEO, Clerk

UK LAND FORCES
13 Clerks
15 Financial Adviser
15 Branch of the Adjutant-General & Quartermaster-General: Major-General IC Administration
16 Secretariat: Colonel, General Staff, GSO II (a), GSO II (b)
16 Branch of the Adjutant-General & Quartermaster-General: DAA & OMG
17 Home Defence Forces: Deputy Air Commander
17 Co-ordination of Air & Ground Staff Action for RAF Home Defence Forces: Chief of Staff
19 Military Adviser, Aide-de-Camp
19 Assistant Military Secretary
20 Naval Operations: Chief Staff Officer
20 Naval Regional Matters, Naval Aid to Civil Power: Staff Officer
20 Logistics: Staff Officer
21 Operation of Aircraft of Home Defence Forces: Logistics: Squadron Leader
21 Staff Officer Group Captain (b), Staff Officer Wing Commander (b), Staff Officer Squadron Leader(b) (i) & (b) (ii)
22 Home Station: Representative
23 Chief of Staff
24 Commander-in-Chief
25 Home Defence Forces: Air Commander
26 Home Defence Forces: Secretary
26 Operation of Aircraft of Home Defence Forces: Signals: Squadron Leader
26 Staff Officer Group Captain (a), Staff Officer Wing Commander (a), Staff Officer Squadron Leader (a) (i) & (a) (ii)

MINISTRY OF HEALTH
27 Assistant Secretary, Principal
29 Minister
30 Private Secretary
31 Permanent Secretary
32 Under-Secretary
33 Deputy Chief Medical Officer
34 Chief Medical Officer
35 Principal Medical Officer
36 Controller of Supplies, Superintending Engineer
37 Clerical & Typing

MINISTRY OF HOUSING & LOCAL GOVERNMENT
38 Map Room
39 Care of the Homeless: Local Government & Related Questions: Principal, Assistant Secretary
39 Water: Principal, Assistant Secretary
40 General Office
40 Water: Personal Assistant
40 Chief Engineer's Personal Assistant
40 Care of the Homeless: Local Government & Related Questions: Personal Assistant
41 Under-Secretary, Chief Engineer
42 Water: Senior Engineering Inspector, Senior Radiochemlcal Inspector
45 Private Secretary, Assistant Private Secretary
46 Deputy Secretary
47 Minister

SCOTTISH OFFICE
48 Permanent Under-Secretary of State
49 Scottish Home Department: Principal, Assistant Secretary
49 Department of Health for Scotland: Assistant Secretary
51 Department of Agriculture & Fisheries for Scotland: Assistant Secretary
52 Department of Agriculture & Fisheries for Scotland: Clerk/Secretaries

LORD ADVOCATE'S DEPARTMENT
51 Legal Secretary (or Deputy)
52 Clerk/Secretary

CENTRAL OFFICE OF INFORMATION
54 Press
55 Secretarial
56 Director General

BRITISH BROADCASTING CORPORATION
57 BBC Control Room
58 BBC Director, Senior BBC Output Staff, Senior BBC Engineering Staff
59 BBC Studio

The central and eastern sections of Area 15 consisted of vacant space earmarked for use as dormitories. Accommodation was provided at the west end for the Camp Commandant and his staff, who were responsible for the day-to-day running of the CGWHQ. Public address and other internal communications systems were also located in this area. Area 16 was occupied by various Home Departments, most important amongst them the Home Defence Secretariat. Until the early 1980s other offices in this area were allocated to the higher administration of UKLF, prior to its temporary move to a dedicated underground bunker at Sopley in Hampshire and thence to Wilton near Salisbury.

Above: The guard-room at the entrance to Area 15. Attached to the wall behind the reception desk are key presses containing the keys to offices in areas 8-12, 19, 21 and 22. Keys for areas 1-7, 17,18 and 20 (all those areas abandoned after 1968) were kept in easily accessible key presses mounted on the wall outside Area 15 on South Main Road.

Above: The public address system in Area 15. This equipment was probably installed by the Ministry of Aircraft Production during the Second World War and was adapted for use in the CGWHQ. The amplifier racks are on the left-hand panel with the power supply unit, radio tuner and a record deck on the racks facing the camera.

Above: Detail view of the valve-driven amplifiers for the public address system.

Above: The Lamson tube exchange. This pneumatic tube system enabled documents, in cylindrical
piston-like containers, to be transferred quickly and securely between offices over considerable distances.
The vertical tubes are for document despatch, the curved, open chutes are for arriving containers.

Above: Detail view of the Lamson tubes showing room allocations.

Below: Lamson containers. Note the airtight end seals. The numbered brass rings can be adjusted to indicate the ultimate destination of the document.

Right: A container ready for despatch via tube No.16.

Left: Tubes from the Lamson exchange suspended from the roof of East First Avenue heading towards the junction with South Main Road.

Below left: Electrically driven compressor and vacuum pumps providing the motive power for the Lamson tube system.

Below right: The Lamson terminal in room 11 in Area 15, which is the CGWHQ central post room. Important documents could be distributed from this room quickly and securely to their destinations without human intervention.

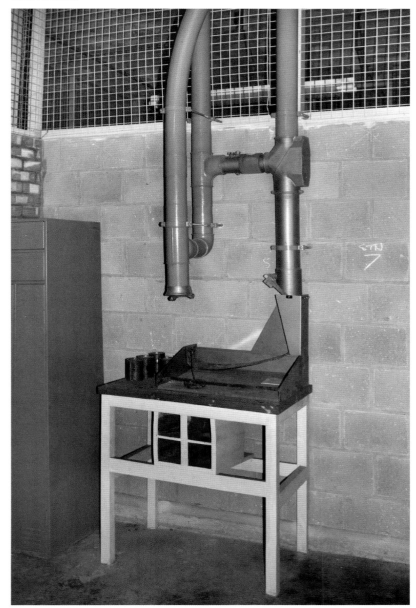

Above and opposite: BBC studio and control room in Area 16. According to a BBC document issued in 1959, the role of this installation was 'to provide instruction, information and encouragement as practicable by means of guidance, news and diversion to relieve stress and strain.'

The secrecy surrounding the Corsham CGWHQ had repercussions for the BBC. An engineering memo issued during the planning stage commented: 'It will be necessary, of course, to provide lines to connect STOCKWELL to the BBC emergency headquarters and distribution point at Wood Norton, but their cost cannot be estimated owing to the lack of information as to the whereabouts of STOCKWELL.'

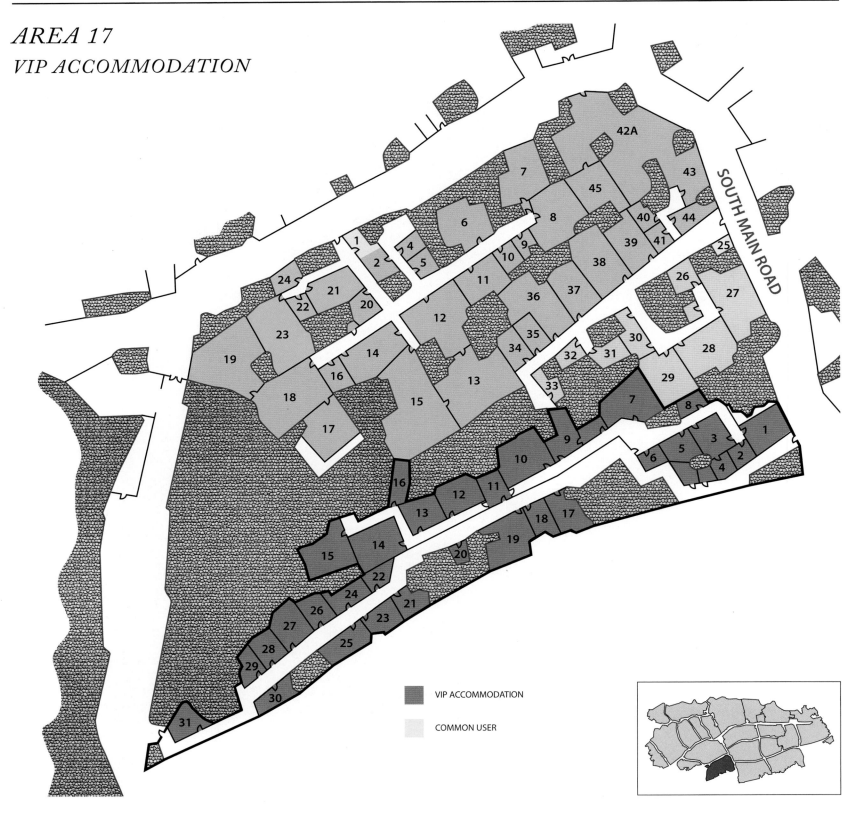

AREA 17
VIP ACCOMMODATION

SOUTH MAIN ROAD

■ VIP ACCOMMODATION

□ COMMON USER

The greater part of the northern section of Area 17, adjacent to the South West Ring Road, was occupied by various elements of UKLF, together with a few offices allocated to the fairly unimportant Ministries of Aviation and Labour. After the 1968 organisation all this accommodation was abandoned and, in the absence of adequate ventilation and air-conditioning, has deteriorated significantly due to the dual problems of high ambient humidity and ground water seepage.

The most intriguing aspect of Area 17, however, is the self-contained, isolated suite of rooms to the south of the area accessible only via an inconspicuous door giving discrete access, via emergency exit door 'C', to goods lift GL3 and thence to the surface. This area, referred to obliquely as the 'VIP accommodation', has been the subject of much speculation since its existence became more widely known in 2004. Although the government has always refused to comment on the arrangements made for the Royal Family in event of war there is evidence that the VIP accommodation in Area 17 was prepared for this purpose.

During the early planning phase for the CGWHQ there appears to have been no specific proposals for the accommodation of the Sovereign and Royal Family, despite the constitutional necessity of Royal Assent in certain pivotal aspects of the government decision-making process. There was a hint in a hand-written note amongst a file of Cabinet Office papers, scribbled in 1959, to the effect that it might have been possible to accommodate a Royal Party of up to twenty-five members in the CGWHQ, but no other concrete reference from that time. In 1961 it was noted that 'in the event of a crisis, the Queen would accompany her government,' which perhaps

implies that she would, in fact, accompany it to Corsham, but this is not expanded upon. Two years later a similarly vaguely phrased memorandum comments that in an emergency 'members of the Royal Family other than the Queen and Heir Apparent' would disperse to various country houses, which again suggests that special provision had been made for the Sovereign. More details of the plans for the Royal Family came to light with the release of documents relating to a scheme developed in 1964, code-named CANDID. Although the documents go into great length detailing the military units that will accompany the Queen and other members of the Royal Family to their places of refuge, there is no mention of the chosen locations. All that is clear is that at that time it was likely that for reasons of safety and survival, the family would be dispersed.

The final, and most substantive, indication regarding the likely refuge for the Royal Family appears in another hand-written document discovered in a file concerned with the planning of the early 1980s incarnation of the reduced-area ALBATROSS scheme. The document lists the various members of the advance party that would depart for Corsham during the warning period. At the top of the list is a group of eight VVIPs – not VIPs but Very, Very Important Persons – accompanied by ten Personal Secretaries. These numbers are a good fit both for the then Royal Family (eight members including the Queen, Prince Philip, Princess Margaret, Queen Elizabeth the Queen Mother, and the Queen's four children), and the accommodation available in Area 17. The ten Personal Secretaries would be accommodated in rooms 21 to 30 located on the outer corridor, with the senior Royals at the east end of the inner sanctum and the younger members in rooms 12 to 15 to the west.

KEY TO AREA 17

UK LAND FORCES
2 Department of the Judge Advocate General, Clerk
3 Deputy Director of Supplies & Transport
4 Deputy Director of Ordnance Services
5 Deputy Director of Electrical & Mechanical Engineers
6 Maintenance, Reserves, Stores, Stocks: DAQMG (c), DAQMG (d)
6 Operations: AQMG, DAQMG (a) & DAQM (b)
7 Maintenance, Reserves, Stores, Stocks: AQMG, DAQMG (a), SC (a), DAQMG (b), SC (b)
8 Maintenance, Reserves, Stores, Stocks: Clerks
9 Assistant Director of Public Relations, Clerks
10 Quartermaster-General's Branch: Brigadier Q
11 Ordnance: ADOS
11 Supplies & Transport: ADST, DADST (a) & DADST (b)
12 Movements: Col. Q. Mov., DAQMG (a) & SC (b)
13 Movements: Clerks
14 Medical: ADMS, DADMS (a), DADMS (b), ADAH
15 Medical: Clerks
15 Supplies & Transport: Clerks

16 Deputy Director of Medical Services
18 Operations: Clerks
19 Ordnance: Clerk
19 Electrical & Mechanical Engineers: Clerk
19 Chaplains: Clerk
20 Deputy Chaplain-General, Chaplain (RC)
34 Deputy Provost Marshal, DAPM
35 Deputy Adjutant General
36 Manpower, Establishment: Clerks
36 Provost: Clerks
37 Personnel Administration: DAAG (a), SC (a)
37 Manpower, Establishment: DAAG (b)
38 Traffic Officer, Cypher NCOs
39 Clerks
40 Supervising Officer
41 Logistics Clerks
42 Admiral's Secretary
44 Nuclear Ground Defence Staff: Group Captain, Wing Commander, Squadron Leader

MINISTRY OF AVIATION
21 Civil Aviation
22 Chief Scientist
23 Supply (Aircraft, Electronics, and Guided Weapons)
24 Deputy Secretary

MINISTRY OF LABOUR
26 Minister
27 General Questions (Organisation of the Ministry): Under-Secretary, Assistant
27 Employment Department & Military Recruitment Department: Under-Secretary, Assistant
28 Industrial Relations Department: Under-Secretary, Assistant
28 Private Secretary
29 British Employers Confederation Representative, Trade Union Congress Representative
30 Permanent Secretary

*Plan showing the layout of the
rooms in the VIP accommodation.*

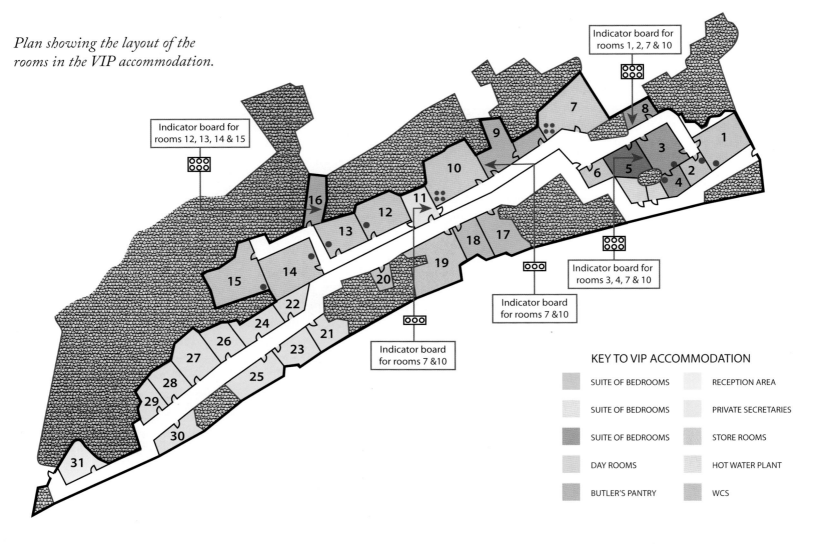

Indicator board for
rooms 1, 2, 7 & 10

Indicator board for
rooms 12, 13, 14 & 15

Indicator board for
rooms 3, 4, 7 & 10

Indicator board
for rooms 7 &10

Indicator board
for rooms 7 &10

KEY TO VIP ACCOMMODATION

SUITE OF BEDROOMS	RECEPTION AREA
SUITE OF BEDROOMS	PRIVATE SECRETARIES
SUITE OF BEDROOMS	STORE ROOMS
DAY ROOMS	HOT WATER PLANT
BUTLER'S PANTRY	WCS

The key to understanding the function of the VIP accommodation in Area 17 is the arrangement of the bell-pushes and indicator panels in the various rooms. Rooms 1 and 2 comprise a bedroom and bathroom suite, both of which have bell-pushes communicating with an indicator in room 8 which it must be assumed is an attendant's room. The indicator panel in room 8 also receives summonses from buttons in rooms 7 and 10, which probably would have functioned as day-rooms. Rooms 3 and 4 comprise a second bedroom and bathroom suite, with communicating buttons to attendant's room 5, which is also in communication with the day-rooms. Room 9 and its adjacent annexe contained limited catering facilities and probably comprised a server or possibly a butler's pantry. It is in communication with day-rooms 7 and 10. To the west of security or reception room number 11 there is a suite of four bedrooms (nos 12 to 15) all of which communicate with attendant's room number 16. Rooms 7 and 10 each have a group of four push-buttons that enable communication with staff in rooms 5, 8, 9 and 11.

The VIP accommodation has three unique features that differentiate it from the rest of the CGWHQ. First, all the room partitions are solid from floor to ceiling, whereas elsewhere they are only seven feet high, the upper sections being completed as simple steel-mesh panels for reasons of economy and to facilitate ventilation. Secondly, rooms 2 and 4 contain the only baths in the complex other than the lone example in the hospital. Finally, room number 1 is heavily reinforced with rolled steel joists and concrete beams providing very substantial overhead protection.

Right: Fragment of a hand-written note, filed in 1982, referring to the eight 'VVIPs' included in the PERIPHERAL advance party.

Below: Room number 11, the reception and security office. The dark passageway on the right leads to the principal accommodation suite, rooms 1-10. The open door just visible to the far right of the photograph leads into the outer access corridor.

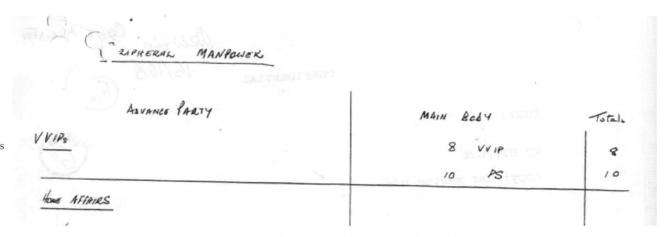

PERIPHERAL	MANPOWER			
	ADVANCE PARTY	MAIN BODY		Total
VVIPs		8	VVIP	8
		10	PS	10
HOME AFFAIRS				

N54ᶜ

Above: Room number 4, the en-suite bathroom attached to room number 3.

Right: Bedroom number 3 with the en-suite bathroom beyond. Note the call-button on the wall, there is another in the bathroom.

Below: Call-indicator in attendant's room number 5 responding to calls from rooms 3, 4, 7 and 10.

Left: Room number 1. This is the most heavily protected room in the whole of the CGWHQ. Notice the additional overhead protection provided by the pre-stressed reinforced concrete beams supported by rolled-steel joists. Staff at Corsham assumed that had the Royal Family been accommodated there then this would have served as the Sovereign's bedroom.

Below left and right: Room number 2, the toilet and bathroom associated with room number 1. Both were provided with call-buttons linked to attendant's room number 8.

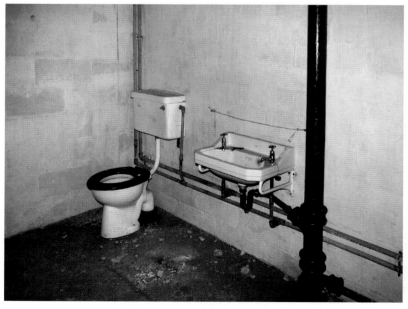

Above: Room number 9, the butler's pantry with sink and work-top.

Above left: Four-way call-button in room number 7.

Middle left: Call-indicator in room number 9, responding to calls from rooms 7 and 10.

Below left: Call-indicator in room number 16 responding to calls from rooms 12, 13, 14 and 15.

WEST MAIN ROAD

PL1

SOUTH WEST RING ROAD

Area 18 is one of the areas which existed only as a concept. Although a theoretical, partial allocation of rooms was made in the early 1960s and the shells of the offices partitioned, none were ever fitted out. By 1968 the original SUBTERFUGE scheme, with its top-heavy, over-centralised manning levels, had been abandoned and, along with it, the whole of Area 18. What remains is now just a maze of mouldering corridors and offices and rotting timberwork. A study of surviving drawings of the area indicate that

KEY TO AREA 18

AIR MINISTRY
8 Registry Telegrams Staff
25 Civil Establishment: Executive Officer
26 Civil Establishment: CEO
27 Organisation & Supply: Chief of Staff
28 Organisation & Supply: Personal Assistant
   to Chief of Staff
29 Civil Establishment: Assistant Secretary
30 Civil Establishment: Principal
31 Civil Establishment: CEO
32 Registry: Typing & Duplicating Pool
33 Registry Telegrams Staff
34 Saceur Liaison: Group Captain, Wing Commander
36 Transport Operations: Wing Commander,
   Squadron Leader
37 Saclant Liaison: Air Commodore
38 Policy & Overseas Operations: Group Captain
39 Policy & Overseas Operations: Air Staff Clerks
40 Policy & Overseas Operations: Wing Commander
41 Saclant Liaison: Wing Commander
42 Secretariat: Under-Secretary B
43 Air Staff Secretariat: Assistant Secretary
44 Deterrent: Wing Commander
45 Deterrent: Group Captain
46 RAF Commander
47 Chief of Air Staff
48 Air Staff Secretariat: Principal, Executive Officer
49 CAS & RAF Commander: Principal, Wing Commander
50 Secretariat: Personal Assistant to Deputy Secretary
51 Secretariat: Deputy Secretary
52 Supply & Organisation Secretariat: Assistant Secretary
53 Supply & Organisation Secretariat: Principal,
   Executive Officer
54 Logistics: Air Commodore
55 Logistics: Group Captain
56 Registry: Executive Officer, Clerical Officer
57 Communications: Group Captain
58 Communications: Wing Commander
59 Communications: Wing Commander
60 Organisation & Works: Wing Commander
60 Administration Plans: Squadron Leader
61 Organisation & Works: Air Commodore
62 Communications: Clerks
63 Organisation & Works: Squadron Leader,
   Wing Commander
64 Technical: Group Captain, Wing Commander
65 Secretariat: Under-Secretary A
66 Logistics: Wing Commander, Squadron Leader

ADMIRALTY
68 Signals (Captain RN)
69 Private Secretary to First Sea Lord
70 Naval Assistant to First Sea Lord
71 Operations (RN)

72 First Sea Lord
73 Deputy Chief Naval Staff
74 Secretary to Deputy Chief Naval Staff
75 Plans (Captain RN)
76 Conference Room
77 Local Display Room
78 Local Display Room
79 Naval Staff
80 Permanent Secretary/Deputy
80A Marine Salvage
81 Private Secretary to Permanent Secretary
82 Naval Staff
83 Principal
84 Naval Personnel Liaison Team
85 Clerical/Typing Pool
86 Under-Secretary
87 Assistant Director of Stores
88 Deputy Director of Victualling
89 Director-General Navy Works & MSR Advisers
91 Controller's Team
92 Controller's Team
93 Controller's Team
94 Supply Team and Movements
94A Naval Accounting & Naval Information
95 Assistant Director Armament Supply
96 Clerical/Typing Pool
97 Clerical/Typing Pool
98 Assistant Secretary
99 Messengers

UNITED KINGDOM LAND FORCES
100 Signals: Chief Signal Officer
103 Operations & Intelligence: GSO II
103 Resources: GSO II
104 Chief Clerk, Clerks
105 Air Support & Supply Drops: GSO II (Air)
105 Current Operations in Area of Attack:
   GSO II (a) (i), GSO II (a) (ii)
105 Operations of Formations/Units Outside
   Area of Attack:
   GSO II (b) (i), GSO II (b) (ii)
106 Operations: GSO I
106 Staff Duties: GSO I
107 Establishments, Organisation, GS Aspects of
   Vehicles, Ammunition, Weapons, Co-ordination:
   GSO II (a), GSO II (b)
107: Manpower Planning & Accounting, Order of
   Battle, Location Statements, Mobilisation, Moves
108 Communication Equipment: SO III
109 Static Communication Plans SO II
109 Liaison Long Line Agency: SO II
110 Branch Co-ordination: GSO II
110 SD, Ops, Manpower: GSO II
111 Communication Equipment: Clerks

112 Resources: Clerks
113 Engineers: GSO I
114 Plans: Clerks
114 Establishments, Organisation, GS Aspects of
   Vehicles, Ammunition, Weapons, Co-ordination: Clerks
115 Liaison Security: Clerks
116 Intelligence: GSO I, GSO II, GSO III
116 Liaison Security: GSO II
117 Plans: GSO II (a), GSO II (b)
118 Plans: GSO I
119 Brigadier, General Staff
120 Chief Engineer

WAR OFFICE
122 Vice-Chief of the Imperial General Staff
123 Chief of the Imperial General Staff
124 Brigadier General Staff, Assistant Director Survey
125 MA/CIGS, MA/VCIGS
126 Clerks to CIGS & MO
127 Directorate of Military Operations - Officers
128 Director of Military Operations
129 Director of Military Intelligence
130 Department of the Permanent Under-Secretary of State
131 Department of the Permanent Under-Secretary of State
132 Clerks to MI & Survey
134 Department of the Permanent Under-Secretary of State
135 Department of the Permanent Under-Secretary of State
136 Under-Secretary of State for War
136A Clerk
138 Department of the Master-General of Ordnance
139 Department of the Permanent Under-Secretary of State
140 Department of the Permanent Under-Secretary of State
141 Directorate of Staff Duties - Officers
142 Directorate of Staff Duties - Officers
143 Signals - Officers
144 Signals - Officers
145 Co-ordinating Branch - Deputy Chief of the
   Imperial General Staff
146 Clerks to DSD, Signals, and E in C
147 Signals - Officers
164 Department of the Quarter-Master-General
165 Department of the Quarter-Master-General
167 Department of the Quarter-Master-General
168 Clerks
169 Engineer-in-Chief - Officers
169 Department of the Quarter-Master-General
170 Department of the Quarter-Master-General
171 Department of the Quarter-Master-General
172 Department of the Quarter-Master-General
173 Department of the Quarter-Master-General

INFORMATION INCOMPLETE

the distribution of rooms was never properly finalised for the layout and room-numbering is haphazard and, particularly in the Air Ministry section, confusing, where many numbers are duplicated and others missing entirely.

AREA 19
THE POWER HOUSE

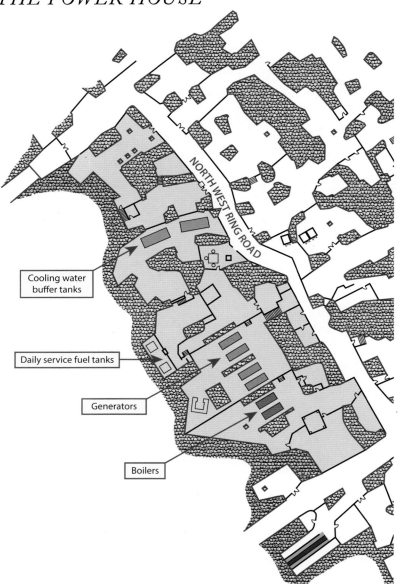

Cooling water buffer tanks

Daily service fuel tanks

Generators

Boilers

Above: One of twelve reserve diesel fuel tanks located in the old workings to the west of Area 1. These tanks held a total of 123,200 gallons of diesel oil.

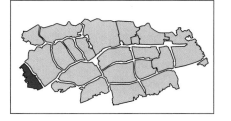

The power house in Area 19 occupies the site of the former factory's No.2 boilerhouse and utilises elements of its infrastructure in its new role. The flue shaft, for example, was modified to carry the generator exhausts to the surface. Four of the original six boilers were removed to make room for four new Mirrlees-engined generator sets. The remaining two survived until the mid-1970s to provide steam for the kitchens and calorifiers but were rendered redundant when a new surface boilerhouse was commissioned to supply both the CGWHQ and adjacent storage depot.

Opposite below: 'Daily service' fuel tank located in the power house. Replenished from the reserve tanks above, this would hold sufficient fuel to run one generator for twenty-four hours.

Above: Two of the four Mirrlees JVSS12 12-cylinder alternator sets installed in the power house. The Mirrlees engines were inadequately cooled and demonstrated a tendency to overheat under sustained load. The construction of a second water storage lagoon outside the secure perimeter of Area 11 in 1982 was, in part, an attempt to relieve this problem.

Above: The four generator sets occupy the locations of four of the steam boilers in the former Spring Quarry No.2 boilerhouse. The two surviving but disused boilers are visible in the background. The steel girders let into the floor to the left of this photograph once supported the generator control panels, dismantled in 1982 in anticipation of the transfer to new locations of the generators under the subsequently aborted ALBATROSS scheme.

Above: Rear view of numbers 1 and 2 generators. Note the twin turbochargers on each unit, one for each bank of cylinders. The vertical blue cylinders are high-pressure air receivers supplying compressed air at approximately 350 psi to start the diesel engines. Integral water pumps maintained a constant flow of coolant through the engine water-jackets, pumped from the lagoon at the east end of the CGWHQ. Hot water was either returned to the lagoon or, if the temperature was too high, was directed instead via a diversion valve to spray nozzles located in ventilation shaft B3, which acted as a makeshift cooling tower.

Above: The two surviving boilers with their fire-tubes blanked-off and boiler fittings removed. Converted from coal to oil firing in the 1950s, these boilers remained in use to supply steam for the kitchens until the mid-1970s when their function was usurped by a new boilerhouse built on the surface to serve both the CGWHQ and the adjacent Admiralty storage depot.

AREA 20
INDUSTRIAL LAUNDRY

Washing machines

Spin dryers

Tumble dryer

Presses

Escalator 'C'

Goods Lift 1

SOUTH WEST RING ROAD

150 151 152 153 155 156 157 158 159 160 161 162

KEY TO AREA 20

WAR OFFICE
150-162   Department of the Adjutant-General

UNALLOCATED

LAUNDRY

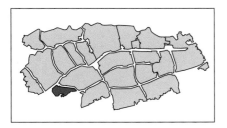

Area 20 housed the CGWHQ laundry and was originally fitted-out with three industrial-scale versions of each of the necessary appliances: washing machines, spin dryers, tumble dryers and steam-heated blanket presses. The laundry would have been used to process bedding and catering linen, rather than personal clothing which would have been the wearer's responsibility to hand-wash in the ablution blocks. In 1968 the laundry was abandoned and one of each type of machine transferred to Area 12 where a smaller-scale facility was established.

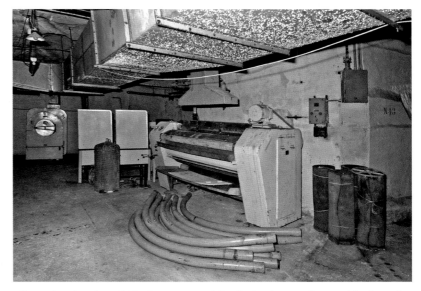

Above: An abandoned blanket press and, in the background, a tumble dryer, in the old industrial laundry. Also visible in this view are a pair of electric ovens removed from the nearby west kitchen and, in front of the press, a pile of spare Lamson tube components.

Above: This view of the laundry shows four rinsing tubs to the left with a Zonda tumble dryer just visible in a bay beyond. Behind the items of kitchen equipment removed from Area 7 and inexplicably dumped here can just be made out a steam-heated blanket press with a similar press to the right. A third press, subsequently transferred to Area 12, resided in the bay in the far right background. On the right are two of the original three Thomas Bradford spin dryers, the third having also been moved to Area 12.

Opposite: Three Thomas Bradford 'Corrujet 65' front-loading industrial washing machines in the disused laundry. A fourth machine, later moved to Area 12, was in a bay to the left of this photograph.

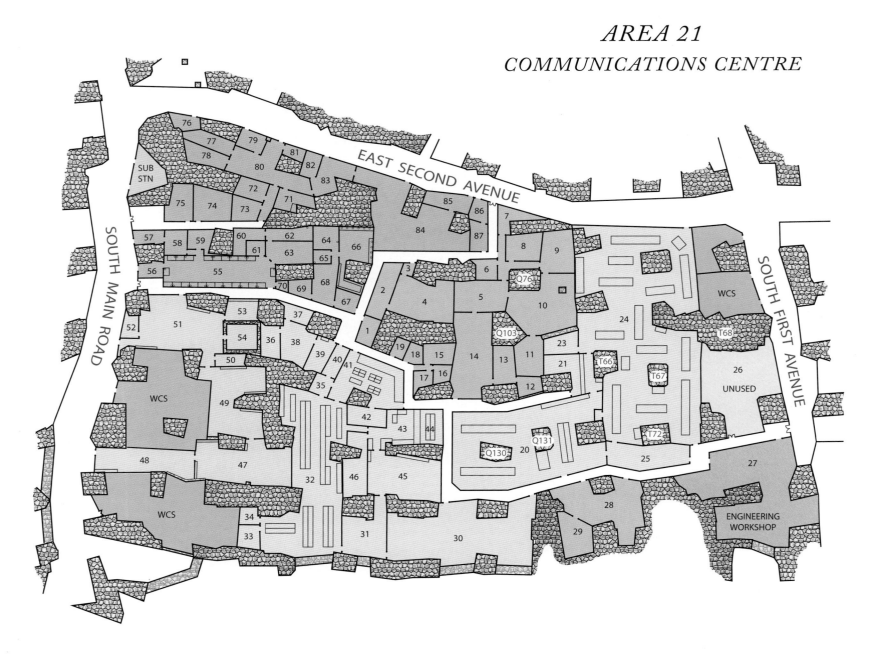

AREA 21
COMMUNICATIONS CENTRE

EAST SECOND AVENUE

SOUTH MAIN ROAD

SOUTH FIRST AVENUE

SUB STN

WCS

WCS

WCS

UNUSED

ENGINEERING WORKSHOP

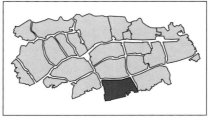

Together with the War Cabinet section directly adjacent to the north, Area 21 was the most important facility serving the CGWHQ. Within this area was concentrated the hub of a complex, encyphered communications system that spanned the globe. Much of the available bandwidth was dedicated to the telegraphic (or teleprinter) links to British overseas diplomatic posts, upon which the government came increasingly to realise it must depend for organising supplies of food and fuel. In the PYTHON era this role came increasingly to the fore as the military requirements were transferred elsewhere.

KEY TO AREA 21

GROUP 1 (WAR CABINET)
1 Tube Exchange
2 Typing & Duplicating Room
3 Messengers Lobby
4 Message Centre, Officer-in-Charge
5 Cypher Office
6 Telephone Secrecy Room
7 Store Room
8 Teleprinter Conference Room B
9 Teleprinter Conference Room A
10 Apparatus Room
11 Battery Room
12 Strong Room
13 Special Store Room
14 Teleprinter Room
15 Chief of Cypher Office, Signal Officer, Custodian & Supply Officer
16 Head of Office, Assistant to Head of Office
17 Staff Clerical Officer, Office Clerks
18 Duty Signal Staff Officers
19 Chief Signal Officer

COMMON USER
20 Teleprinters
21 Teleprinters, Messenger Waiting Room
22 Teleprinters
23 Teleprinters, Store
24 Teleprinters
25 Officer-in-Charge, Enquiries
30 Overseas Telephone & Telegraph Control Equipment
31 Post Office

REST ROOMS
28 PO & Group 5 Joint Rest Rooms
29 PO & Group 5 Joint Rest Rooms

GROUP 5 (WAR OFFICE/ HOME OFFICE & CIVIL DEPARTMENTS)
32 Traffic Hall, Out Traffic Supervisor, In Traffic Supervisor, Patching Panel
33 Teleprinter Switchboard Room
34 Apparatus Room
35 Chief Duty Signal Officer
36 Scrutiny Section
37 Head of Message Centre
38 Classified & Unclassified Section
39 Distribution & Reproduction, Group 5 Pneumatic Tubes
40 Chief Duty Signal Officer-Clerks, Statistics & Records
41 Counter Room & Counter Room Supervisor
42 File & Re-Run Section

43 Off-Line Cypher
44 Stationery
45 Off-Line Cypher, Workshop
46 Chief Cypher Officer

GROUP 4 (FOREIGN OFFICE/ COMMONWEALTH RELATIONS OFFICE/ COLONIAL OFFICE)
47 Machine Cypher Room
48 Teleprinter Room
49 Book Cypher Room
50 Chief Signals Officer
51 Message Centre
52 Typist
53 Wireless Room
54 Strong Room

GROUP 3 (AIR MINISTRY)
55 Traffic Hall
56 Cloaks
57 RAF CO
58 WO & Orderly Room
59 Crypto Workshop
60 Crypto Equipment Room
61 Duty Signal Master
62 Checking & Filing Office
63 Traffic Office
64 In & Out Hatches
65 Distribution
66 Off-Line Crypto
67 Message Reception
68 Head of Watch
69 Head of Registry Telegrams
70 Line Relay Room

GROUP 2 (ADMIRALTY)
71 Message & Filing Room
72 Crypto Officer
73 Crypto Workshop
74 Top Secret Crypto Officer
75 On-Line Cypher Room
76 Stationery Store
77 Perforating Room
78 Duplicating Room
79 Officer-in-Charge
80 Main Signal Office
81 Messengers
82 Duty Signal Officer
83 Routing Room
84 A/T Room
85 Workshop, Ready Use Store
86 Equipment Room
87 T/P Conference Room
88 Message & Filing Room

Above right: The massive vault door of the Foreign Office strong room (room 54), severely corroded and now impossible to open.

Below right: Detail view showing the poor condition of the rotary combination lock securing the door to the Foreign Office strong room.

Left and above right: General views of room 24, the common-user teleprinter room. The communications centre employed over 700 teleprinters of various types, mainly variations on the Creed Model 7 in the early days until these were superseded, in part, by all-in-one Creed Type 444 machines.

Below: Examples of some of the types of equipment to be found in the teleprinter room including, from left to right on the bench, a Creed Type 6S tape reader/transmitter, a Type 7 teleprinter and a Type 45 off-line perforator.

Above: Room 21, the common-user messenger's waiting room. The instruments on the counter top are GNT Undulators *(see page 212)*. Note the Lamson tube terminal in the background.

Left: Teleprinters and operator's chairs, unused and in their manufacturer's protective wrapping, stored in a corner of room 20 *(see plan for location)*. Very little of the equipment was properly installed; much was just held in store and in some locations the rotting timber benches have collapsed under the weight of equipment stored on them.

Above left: Room 14, the War Cabinet (Group 1) teleprinter room. The three instruments on the desk, surmounted by red and green indicator lamps, are teleprinter control instruments and would have originally been fitted with conventional telephone-type dials. The lamps indicate whether the connected lines are free or in receipt of outgoing or incoming messages. The grey cabinets below the desk are sound-proof teleprinter enclosures.

Above right: The vault door securing the Cabinet Office section strong room.

Below left: Room 10, the GPO (later British Telecom) apparatus room in the War Cabinet section of the communications centre. It would appear that equipment in this room was in transition at the time of closure.

Above: Room 30, the GPO overseas telephone and telegraph control equipment room.

Above and opposite: Most of the racks in the GPO overseas telephone and telegraph equipment room consists of Voice Frequency (VF) modulators and associated apparatus. Conventional teleprinter machines (and telephones) utilise 17-cycle AC current for signalling, switching and other supervisory functions. This however, is only suitable for short line lengths. Messages transmitted over even moderately long distances require amplification in repeater stations, and it is not possible to amplify the low frequency AC signals. It is necessary, therefore, to modulate the 17-cycle current to Voice Frequency in the speech band in order for it to be handled by the intermediate repeater stations. Other equipment will demodulate incoming VF back to 17-cycle (or whatever is the local standard).

Left: Creed Type 444 teleprinters. These were introduced in 1966 and performed all the functions (tape reader/perforator, printer and transmission keyboard) that had previously been shared amongst a range of separate devices. Here, in a particularly damp section of Area 21, the racking upon which the instruments were stored has rotted and collapsed.

Below left: A Creed Type 45 off-line perforator. With this machine messages would be punched out on paper tape in five-bit Baudot code ready for transmission at a later time.

Below right: GNT Morse code undulator. Morse code is a simple, reliable code that can be transmitted by the most unsophisticated equipment and often gets through when other systems fail. The undulator prints the code directly onto paper tape that is instantly readable by suitably skilled operators.

Opposite above: Creed Type 7B teleprinter.

Opposite below: Creed Type 7TR1 reperforator, used to prepare messages on punched tape.

AREA 22
FOREIGN & COMMONWEALTH
DEPARTMENTS

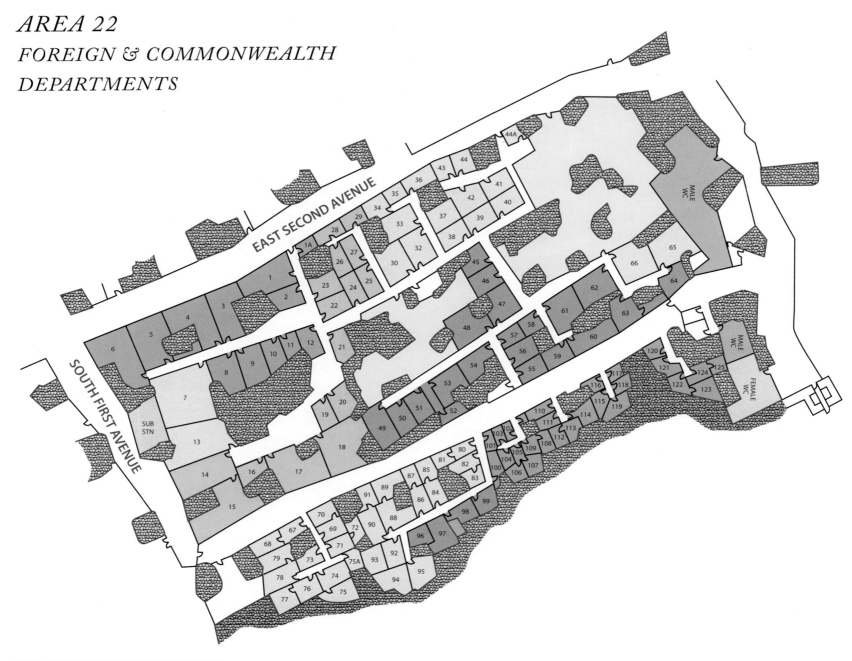

EAST SECOND AVENUE

SOUTH FIRST AVENUE

MALE WC

MALE WC

FEMALE WC

SUB STN

44A

Area 21 was allocated to the group of departments involved with foreign affairs. Its proximity to both the War Cabinet organisation in Area 14 and the communications centre in Area 21 is an indication of the importance attached to these functions. Within this area two groups of rooms, marked as 'unallocated' on the plan above, were reserved for foreign diplomats stranded in the United Kingdom at a time of crisis. Controversially, two suits of rooms (Nos 80-83 and 98-99) were allocated to representatives from the French and United States embassies.

KEY TO AREA 22

COMMONWEALTH RELATIONS OFFICE
1   Reception
2   Parliamentary Under-Secretary of State
3   Typing Section
4   Foreign Affairs: Assistant Secretary/Principal
5   Africa: Assistant Secretary/Principal
5   Economic: Assistant Secretary/Principal
5   Constitutional & General: Assistant Secretary
6   Information: Chief Information Officer
6   Administration: Senior Executive Officer,
     Executive Officer
8   Secretary of State
9   Personal Assistants
9   Co-ordination & Enquiries: Private Secretary, Principal
10   Permanent Under-Secretary of State
11   Deputy Under-Secretary of State
12   Economic: Assistant Under-Secretary of State
12   Administration: Assistant Under-Secretary of State
100-125   Commonwealth High Commissioners

COLONIAL OFFICE
14   Copy Typing & Duplicating
15   Clerical & Shorthand Section
16   Control & Establishments
17   Defence & Intelligence
18   Economic, Supplies and Production
19   Permanent Under-Secretary of State
20   Secretary of State
21   Private Secretaries
22   Private Secretary
23   West Indies
24   Far East & Pacific
25   Under-Secretary of State
26   Mediterranean
27   East & Central Africa
28   Legal Advisor
29   Crown Agents Liaison Officer

FOREIGN OFFICE
45-46   Spare
47   Personal Assistants
48   SE Asia, Far East, Middle East
49   Europe/NATO, Legal Advisor
50   Lord Privy Seal
51   Personal Under-Secretary
52   Deputy Under-Secretary
53   Private Secretaries
54   Secretary of State
55   Interview Room
56   Interview Room
57   Deputy Under-Secretary
58   Deputy Under-Secretary
59   Africa, Latin America
60   General, United Nations
61   Shorthand Typist/Typing Pool
62   E & O Department,
     C & S Department, General
63   Soviet Union, Information Policy,
     Personnel Department
64   Messengers & Stores
80-83   American Embassy
96-97   Spare
98-99   French Embassy

DORMITORIES

UNALLOCATED

Above: Chairs and disassembled iron bedsteads stored under dust sheets in Area 22.

Below: Even for the various Commonwealth High Commissioners living conditions would have been far from comfortable. Here we see a typical example of VIP sleeping accommodation.

BIBLIOGRAPHY

Beard, T and Emmerson A, 2007, *London's Secret Tubes*, Capital Transport Publishing, ISBN: 9781854143112

Campbell, D, 1982, *War Plan UK*, Burnett Books, ISBN: 9780091506711

Campbell, D, 1986, *The Unsinkable Aircraft Carrier*, Grafton Books, ISBN: 9780586086261

Catford, N, 2010, *Cold War Bunkers*, Folly Books, ISBN: 9780956440525

Clarke, R, 1986, *London Under Attack: The Report of the Greater London Area War Risk Study Commission*, Wiley-Blackwell, ISBN: 9780631150442

Cocroft, W D and Thomas, R J C, 2003, *Cold War: Building for Nuclear Confrontation 1946-89*, English Heritage, ISBN: 9781873592816

Fox, S, 2010, *'Top Secret – Acid: The Story of Central Government War Headquarters'*, Subterranea, Issue 22, 1 - 72, ISSN 1741-8917

Hawkins, D, 2011, *Bath Stone Quarries*, Folly Books, ISBN: 9780956440549

Laurie, P, 1979, *Beneath the City Streets*, Panther, ISBN: 9780586050552

McCamley, N J, 1998, *Secret Underground Cities*, 1998, Pen & Sword, ISBN: 9780850527339

McCamley, N J, 2000, *Cold War Secret Nuclear Bunkers*, Pen & Sword, ISBN: 9781844155088

McCamley, N J, 2006, *The Secret History of Chemical Warfare*, Pen & Sword, ISBN: 9781844153411

McCamley, N, 2010, *Second World War Secret Bunkers*, Folly Books, ISBN: 9780956440532

Stokes, P, 1996, *Drakelow Unearthed: The secret history of an underground complex*, BCS/Paul Stokes, ISBN: 9780904015409

Spies for Peace, 1963, *Danger! Official Secret RSG-6*